Meditations
Of
Jesus Christ

Eat My Flesh & Drink My Blood

Dr Michael H Yeager

ISBN:1537169319
ISBN-13:9781537169316

DEDICATION

We dedicate this book to those who also face the dilemma of being human, to those who know what it's like to fall short of the glory and yet keep getting back up and striving by faith. We dedicate this to those who keep pressing towards the mark for the prize of the high calling of God in **Christ Jesus**; fellow believers who are on the journey of life, who stumble but never quit. They just keep getting back up and pressing on. It is only by the supernatural touch of God, the life of **Christ**, by which we are able to accomplish His will.

CONTENTS

ACKNOWLEDGMENTS

All of the Scriptures used in this **meditation book** is from the original 1611 version of the King James Bible. I give thanks to **God the Father , Jesus Christ and the Holy Ghost** for the powerful impact the word has had upon my life. Without the word Quickened in my heart by the **Holy Ghost** I would have been lost and undone. To the **Lord** of Heaven and Earth I am eternally indebted for **His** great love and his mercy, **His** protections and **His** provisions, **His** divine guidance and overwhelming goodness. To **Him** be all of the glory, honor and praise for ever and ever: Amen .

CHAPTER ONE
FOUNDATIONAL SCRIPTURES

There are some basic foundational Scriptures about **JESUS** that you should memorize in order to grasp the reality of God's will revealed in Christ. I would strongly suggest that before you proceed much further in this **meditation book** that you memorize these particular Scriptures and begin to meditate upon them. when I use the word meditate I am referring to speaking them to yourself, muttering over and over slowly allowing the Holy Spirit to quicken these words to your heart. There must be a quickening of the Scriptures in order for there to be faith to bring to pass that which you are speaking. Psalms 119 is a wonderful declaration of the quickening of God's word.

Foundational Scriptures

*John 1:1 In the beginning was the Word, and the Word was with God, and the Word was God. 2 The same was in the beginning with God. 3 All things were made by him; and without him was not anything made that was made. 4 In him was life; and the life was the light of men. 5 And the light shineth in darkness; and the darkness comprehended it not.........10 He was in the world, and the world was made by him, and the world knew him not.11 He came unto his own, and his own received him not.12 But as many as received him, to them gave he power to become the sons of God, even to them that believe on his name:13 Which were born, not of blood, nor of the will of the flesh, nor of the will of man, but of God.14 And the Word was made flesh, and dwelt among us, (and we beheld his glory, the glory as of the only begotten of the Father,) full of grace and truth.

*John 3:19 And this is the condemnation, that light is come into the world, and men loved darkness rather than light, because their deeds were evil.

John 3:36 He that believeth on the Son hath everlasting life: and he that believeth not the Son shall not see life; but the wrath of God abideth on him.

The Eight "I am" statements of Jesus in the gospel of John

John 6: 35, 48 I am the bread of life
John 8: 12, 9:5 I am the light of the world
John 8: 58 Before Abraham was, I am
John 10:9 I am the door
John 10:11 I am the good shepherd
John 11:25 I am the resurrection and the life
John 14:6 I am the way, the truth, and the life
John 15:1 I am the true vine

*John 6:33 For the bread of God is he which cometh down from heaven, and giveth life unto the world.........

*John 6:35 And Jesus said unto them, I am the bread of life: he that cometh to me shall never hunger; and he that believeth on me shall never thirst.................

*John 6:38 For I came down from heaven, not to do mine own will, but the will of him that sent me........

*John 6:40 And this is the will of him that sent me, that everyone which seeth the Son, and believeth on him, may have everlasting life: and I will raise him up at the last day.........

*John 6:44 No man can come to me, except the Father which hath sent me draw him: and I will raise him up at the last day.....

*John 6:47 Verily, verily, I say unto you, He that believeth on me hath everlasting life.48 I am that bread of life.49 Your fathers did eat manna in the wilderness, and are dead.50 This is the bread which cometh down from heaven, that a man may eat thereof, and not die.51 I am the living bread which came down from heaven: if any man eat of this bread, he shall live forever: and the bread that I will give is my flesh, which I will give for the life of the world..

---

*John 6:53 Then Jesus said unto them, Verily, verily, I say unto you, Except ye eat the flesh of the Son of man, and drink his blood, ye have no life in you.54 Whoso eateth my flesh, and drinketh my blood, hath eternal life; and I will raise him up at the last day.55 For my flesh is meat indeed, and my blood is drink indeed.56 He that eateth my flesh, and drinketh my blood, dwelleth in me, and I in him.57 As the living Father hath sent me, and I live by the Father: so he that eateth me, even he shall live by me.58 This is that bread which came down from heaven: not as your fathers did eat manna, and are dead: he that eateth of this bread shall live for ever.....

---

*John 6:63 It is the spirit that quickeneth; the flesh profiteth nothing: the words that I speak unto you, they are spirit, and they are life.

John 7:38 He that believeth on me, as the scripture hath said, out of his belly shall flow rivers of living water.

---

*John 8:12 Then spake Jesus again unto them, saying, I am the light of the world: he that followeth me shall not walk in darkness, but shall have the light of life.

John 9:5 As long as I am in the world, I am the light of the world.

---

*John 10: 9 I am the door: by me if any man enter in, he shall be saved, and shall go in and out, and find pasture.

10 - The thief cometh not, but for to steal, and to kill, and to destroy: I am come that they might have life, and that they might have [it] more abundantly. 11 I am the good shepherd: the good shepherd giveth his life for the sheep.

John 11:25 Jesus said unto her, I am the resurrection, and the life: he that believeth in me, though he were dead, yet shall he live:

---

*John 12:46 I am come a light into the world, that whosoever believeth on me should not abide in darkness.

John 14:6 Jesus saith unto him, I am the way, the truth, and the life: no man cometh unto the Father, but by me.

---

*John 15:I am the true vine, and my Father is the husbandman.2 Every branch in me that beareth not fruit he taketh away: and every branch that beareth fruit, he purgeth it, that it may bring forth more fruit.3 Now ye are clean through the word which I have spoken unto you.4 Abide in me, and I in you. As the branch cannot bear fruit of itself, except it abide in the vine; no more can ye, except ye abide in me.5 I am the vine, ye are the branches: He that abideth in me, and I in him, the same bringeth forth much fruit: for without me ye can do nothing.6 If a man abide not in me, he is cast forth as a branch, and is withered; and men gather them, and cast them into the fire, and they are burned.7 If ye abide in me, and my words abide in you, ye shall ask what ye will, and it shall be done unto you.8 Herein is my Father glorified, that ye bear much fruit; so shall ye be my disciples.9 As the Father hath loved me, so have I loved you: continue ye in my love.10 If ye keep my commandments, ye shall abide in my love; even as I have kept my Father's commandments, and abide in his love.11 These things have I spoken unto you, that my joy might remain in you, and that your joy might be full.

John 15:14 Ye are my friends, if ye do whatsoever I command you.

John 17:21 That they all may be one; as thou, Father, art in me, and I in thee, that they also may be one in us: that the world may believe that thou hast sent me.22 And the glory which thou gavest me I have given them; that they may be one, even as we are one:23 I in them, and thou in me, that they may be made perfect in one; and that the world may know that thou hast sent me, and hast loved them, as thou hast loved me.24 Father, I will that they also, whom thou hast given me, be with me where I am; that they may behold my glory, which thou hast given me: for thou lovedst me before the foundation of the world.25 O righteous Father, the world hath not known thee: but I have known thee, and these have known that thou hast sent me.26 And I have declared unto them thy name, and will declare it: that the love wherewith thou hast loved me may be in them, and I in them.

---

*Proverbs 4:20 My son, attend to my words; incline thine ear unto my sayings.21 Let them not depart from thine eyes; keep them in the midst of thine heart.22 For they are life unto those that find them, and health to all their flesh.

---

*Joshua 1:8 *The reality of Christ* shall not depart out of thy mouth; but thou shalt meditate *upon Him* therein day and night, that thou mayest observe to do according to all that *He has spoken*: for then thou shalt make thy way prosperous, and then thou shalt have good success. 9 Have not I commanded thee? Be strong and of a good courage; be not afraid, neither be thou dismayed: for the Lord thy God (*Jesus Christ*) is with thee whithersoever thou goest.

Loving and Abiding In Christ

Matthew 12:50 For whosoever shall do the will of my Father which is in heaven, the same is my brother, and sister, and mother.

Luke 6:46 And why call ye me, Lord, Lord, and do not the things which I say?

Luke 10:27 And he answering said, Thou shalt love the Lord thy God (*JESUS*) with all thy heart, and with all thy soul, and with all thy strength, and with all thy mind; and thy neighbour as thyself.28 And he said unto him, Thou hast answered right: this do, and thou shalt live.

John 8:31Then said Jesus to those Jews which believed on him, If ye continue in my word, then are ye my disciples indeed;

John14:21 He that hath my commandments, and keepeth them, he it is that loveth me: and he that loveth me shall be loved of my Father, and I will love him, and will manifest myself to him.........

23 Jesus answered and said unto him, If a man love me, he will keep my words: and my Father will love him, and we will come unto him, and make our abode with him.24 He that loveth me not keepeth not my sayings: and the word which ye hear is not mine, but the Father's which sent me.

John 15: 9 As the Father hath loved me, so have I loved you: continue ye in my love. 10 If ye keep my commandments, ye shall abide in my love; even as I have kept my Father's commandments, and abide in his love.

John 16:27 For the Father himself loveth you, because ye have loved me, and have believed that I came out from God.

*1 Corinthians 13:1 Though I speak with the tongues of men and of angels, and have not Love *For CHRIST*, I am become as sounding brass, or a tinkling cymbal.2 And though I have the gift of prophecy, and understand all mysteries, and all knowledge; and though I have all faith, so that I could remove mountains, and have not *Love For CHRIST*, I am nothing.3 And though I bestow all my goods to feed the poor, and though I give my body to be burned, and have not *Love For CHRIST*, it profiteth me nothing.4 *CHRIST* suffereth long, and is kind; CHRIST envieth not; *CHRIST* vaunteth not *HIM* self, is not puffed up,5 Doth not behave *HIM* self unseemly, seeketh not *HIS* own, is not easily provoked, thinketh no evil; 6 *CHRIST* Rejoiceth not in iniquity, but rejoiceth in the truth; 7 *CHRIST* Beareth all things, believeth all things, hopeth all things, endureth all things.8 *CHRIST* will never faileth: but whether there be prophecies, they shall fail; whether there be tongues, they shall cease; whether there be knowledge, it shall vanish away. 9 For we know in part, and we prophesy in part.10 But when *HE* which is perfect is come, then that which is in part shall be done away.11 When I was a child, I spake as a child, I understood as a child, I thought as a child: but when I became a man, I put away childish things.12 For now we see through a glass, darkly; but then face to face: now I know in part; but then shall I know even as also I am known.13 And now abideth faith, hope, *Love For CHRIST*, these three; but the greatest of these is *Love For CHRIST*.

1 Corinthians 16:22 If any man love not the Lord Jesus Christ, let him be Anathema Maranatha.

2 Corinthians 5:14 For the love of Christ constraineth us; because we thus judge, that if one died for all, then were all dead: 15 And that he died for all, that they which live should not

henceforth live unto themselves, but unto him which died for them, and rose again.

Romans 8:28 And we know that all things work together for good to them that love God, to them who are the called according to his purpose.

Galatians 2:20 I am crucified with Christ: nevertheless I live; yet not I, but Christ liveth in me: and the life which I now live in the flesh I live by the faith of the Son of God, who loved me, and gave himself for me.

Ephesians 3:14 For this cause I bow my knees unto the Father of our Lord Jesus Christ,15 Of whom the whole family in heaven and earth is named,16 That he would grant you, according to the riches of his glory, to be strengthened with might by his Spirit in the inner man;17 That Christ may dwell in your hearts by faith; that ye, being rooted and grounded in love,18 May be able to comprehend with all saints what is the breadth, and length, and depth, and height;19 And to know the love of Christ, which passeth knowledge, that ye might be filled with all the fulness of God.20 Now unto him that is able to do exceeding abundantly above all that we ask or think, according to the power that worketh in us,21 Unto him be glory in the church by Christ Jesus throughout all ages, world without end. Amen.

Philippians 3:8 Yea doubtless, and I count all things but loss for the excellency of the knowledge of Christ Jesus my Lord: for whom I have suffered the loss of all things, and do count them but dung, that I may win Christ,9 And be found in him, not having mine own righteousness, which is of the law, but that which is through the faith of Christ, the righteousness which is of God by faith:10 That I may know him, and the power of his resurrection, and the fellowship of his sufferings, being made conformable unto his death;11 If by any means I might attain unto the resurrection of the dead.

James 2:5 Hearken, my beloved brethren, Hath not God chosen the poor of this world rich in faith, and heirs of the kingdom which he hath promised to them that love him?

1 John 1:1 That which was from the beginning, which we have heard, which we have seen with our eyes, which we have looked upon, and our hands have handled, of the Word of life;2 (For the life was manifested, and we have seen it, and bear witness, and shew unto you that eternal life, which was with the Father, and was manifested unto us;)3 That which we have seen and heard declare we unto you, that ye also may have fellowship with us: and truly our fellowship is with the Father, and with his Son Jesus Christ.

1 John 2: 5 But whoso keepeth his word, in him verily is the love of God perfected: hereby know we that we are in him.6 He that saith he abideth in him ought himself also so to walk, even as he walked.

1 John 3:18 My little children, let us not love in word, neither in tongue; but in deed and in truth.19 And hereby we know that we are of the truth, and shall assure our hearts before him.20 For if our heart condemn us, God is greater than our heart, and knoweth all things.21 Beloved, if our heart condemn us not, then have we confidence toward God.22 And whatsoever we ask, we receive of him, because we keep his commandments, and do those things that are pleasing in his sight.23 And this is his commandment, That we should believe on the name of his Son Jesus Christ, and love one another, as he gave us commandment.24 And he that keepeth his commandments dwelleth in him, and he in him. And hereby we know that he abideth in us, by the Spirit which he hath given us.

1 John 5:3 For this is the love of God, that we keep his commandments: and his commandments are not grievous.

2 John 6 And this is love, that we walk after his commandments. This is the commandment, That, as ye have heard from the beginning, ye should walk in it.

Revelation 3:20 Behold, I stand at the door, and knock: if any man hear my voice, and open the door, I will come in to him, and will sup with him, and he with me.

Psalm 73:25Whom have I in heaven but thee? and there is none upon earth that I desire beside thee.

<u>Renewing of the Mind</u>

When you give your heart to **Jesus Christ**, you're born again, washed in the blood, redeemed, a child of God. From this point forward a wonderful transformation will begin to happen as you start renewing your mind with the word of God. The following Scriptures are powerful promises that you should meditate on every day unto the reality of **Christ** overwhelms all your natural surroundings. As your mind is renewed the new creation will step forth in your life and begin to direct and dominate everything you do and say. **Christ will be manifested in you, to you, through you, by you, and for you.**

* Romans 11:36 For of him, and through him, and to him, are all things: to whom be glory forever. Amen. 12:1 I beseech you therefore, brethren, by the mercies of God, that ye present your bodies a living sacrifice, holy, acceptable unto God, which is your reasonable service. 2 And be not conformed to this world: but be ye transformed by the renewing of your mind, that ye may prove what is that good, and acceptable, and perfect, will of God.

Ephesians 4:22 That ye put off concerning the former conversation the old man, which is corrupt according to the deceitful lusts;23 And be renewed in the spirit of your mind;24 And that ye put on the new man, which after God is created in

righteousness and true holiness.

---

*Philippians 2:5 Let this mind be in you, which was also in Christ Jesus: 6 who, being in the form of God, thought it not robbery to be equal with God: 7 but made himself of no reputation, and took upon him the form of a servant, and was made in the likeness of men: 8 and being found in fashion as a man, he humbled himself, and became obedient unto death, even the death of the cross. 9 Wherefore God also hath highly exalted him, and given him a name which is above every name: 10 that at the name of Jesus every knee should bow, of things in heaven, and things in earth, and things under the earth; 11 and that every tongue should confess that Jesus Christ is Lord, to the glory of God the Father.

---

*Philippians 3:3 - For we are the circumcision, which worship God in the spirit, and rejoice in Christ Jesus, and have no confidence in the flesh.

Philippians 4:8 Finally, brethren, whatsoever things are true, whatsoever things are honest, whatsoever things are just, whatsoever things are pure, whatsoever things are lovely, whatsoever things are of good report; if there be any virtue, and if there be any praise, think on these things.9 Those things, which ye have both learned, and received, and heard, and seen in me, do: and the God of peace shall be with you.

Colossians 3:9 Lie not one to another, seeing that ye have put off the old man with his deeds;10 And have put on the new man, which is renewed in knowledge after the image of him that created him:

---

*James 1:21 wherefore lay apart all filthiness and superfluity of naughtiness, and receive with meekness the engrafted word, which is able to save your souls.

*2 Timothy 3:16 All scripture is given by inspiration of God, and is profitable for doctrine, for reproof, for correction, for instruction in righteousness:17 That the man of God may be perfect, thoroughly furnished unto all good works.

*Psalm 19:7 The law of the Lord is perfect, converting the soul: the testimony of the Lord is sure, making wise the simple.

*Psalm 23:3 He restoreth my soul: he leadeth me in the paths of righteousness for his name's sake.

Psalm 103:5 Who satisfieth thy mouth with good things; so that thy youth is renewed like the eagle's.

Isaiah 40:31 But they that wait upon the Lord shall renew their strength; they shall mount up with wings as eagles; they shall run, and not be weary; and they shall walk, and not faint.

<u>Christ the Perfect Will of God</u>

God is diligently searching for those who will simply be in agreement with him. What happened is that when man partook of sin he was put out of harmony with God. **Jesus Christ was one with the Father, in word, deed and action.** He boldly declared that if you hear me you hear the Father. The words he spoke he declared were not his but the Fathers. Even the works that he did were not of him but from the Father. The last words we hear Christ pray before he went to the garden of Gethsemane were: *Father make them one with us even as we are one!*

John 3:32 And what he hath seen and heard, that he testifieth; and no man receiveth his testimony.33 He that hath received his

testimony hath set to his seal that God is true.34 For he whom God hath sent speaketh the words of God: for God giveth not the Spirit by measure unto him.

John 5:17 But Jesus answered them, My Father worketh hitherto, and I work.

John 5:19 Then answered Jesus and said unto them, Verily, verily, I say unto you, The Son can do nothing of himself, but what he seeth the Father do: for what things so ever he doeth, these also doeth the Son likewise.

John 6:38 For I came down from heaven, not to do mine own will, but the will of him that sent me.39 And this is the Father's will which hath sent me, that of all which he hath given me I should lose nothing, but should raise it up again at the last day.40 And this is the will of him that sent me, that everyone which seeth the Son, and believeth on him, may have everlasting life: and I will raise him up at the last day.

John 7:28 Then cried Jesus in the temple as he taught, saying, Ye both know me, and ye know whence I am: and I am not come of myself, but he that sent me is true, whom ye know not.29 But I know him: for I am from him, and he hath sent me.

John 7:16 Jesus answered them, and said, My doctrine is not mine, but his that sent me.

John 8:28 Then said Jesus unto them, When ye have lifted up the Son of man, then shall ye know that I am he, and that I do nothing of myself; but as my Father hath taught me, I speak these things.

John 8:38 I speak that which I have seen with my Father: and ye do that which ye have seen with your father.

John 10:30 I and my Father are one.

John 10: 37 If I do not the works of my Father, believe me not.38 But if I do, though ye believe not me, believe the works: that ye may know, and believe, that the Father is in me, and I in him.

John 12:49 For I have not spoken of myself; but the Father which sent me, he gave me a commandment, what I should say, and what I should speak.

John 14:9 Jesus saith unto him, Have I been so long time with you, and yet hast thou not known me, Philip? he that hath seen me hath seen the Father; and how sayest thou then, Show us the Father?10 Believest thou not that I am in the Father, and the Father in me? the words that I speak unto you I speak not of myself: but the Father that dwelleth in me, he doeth the works.

John 14:20 At that day ye shall know that I am in my Father, and ye in me, and I in you.

John 17:8 For I have given unto them the words which thou gavest me; and they have received them, and have known surely that I came out from thee, and they have believed that thou didst send me.

2 Corinthians 4:6 For God, who commanded the light to shine out of darkness, hath shined in our hearts, to give the light of the knowledge of the glory of God in the face of Jesus Christ.7 But we have this treasure in earthen vessels, that the excellency of the power may be of God, and not of us.

2 Corinthians 5:19 To wit, that God was in Christ, reconciling the world unto himself, not imputing their trespasses unto them;

and hath committed unto us the word of reconciliation.

Colossians 1:15 Who is the image of the invisible God, the firstborn of every creature:16 For by him were all things created, that are in heaven, and that are in earth, visible and invisible, whether they be thrones, or dominions, or principalities, or powers: all things were created by him, and for him:17 And he is before all things, and by him all things consist.

*Colossians 3:17 - And whatsoever ye do in word or deed, [do] all in the name of the Lord Jesus, giving thanks to God and the Father by him.

*Hebrews 1:1 God, who at sundry times and in divers manners spake in time past unto the fathers by the prophets, 2 hath in these last days spoken unto us by his Son, whom he hath appointed heir of all things, by whom also he made the worlds; 3 who being the brightness of his glory, and the express image of his person, and upholding all things by the word of his power, when he had by himself purged our sins, sat down on the right hand of the Majesty on high;

Hebrews 10:6 In burnt offerings and sacrifices for sin thou hast had no pleasure.7 Then said I, Lo, I come (in the volume of the book it is written of me,) to do thy will, O God.

Hebrews 12:1 Wherefore seeing we also are compassed about with so great a cloud of witnesses, let us lay aside every weight, and the sin which doth so easily beset us, and let us run with patience the race that is set before us,2 Looking unto Jesus the author and finisher of our faith; who for the joy that was set before him endured the cross, despising the shame, and is set down at the right hand of the throne of God.3 For consider him that endured such contradiction of sinners against himself, lest ye be wearied and faint in your minds.4 Ye have not yet resisted unto blood, striving against sin.

*1 Peter 3:12 For the eyes of the Lord are over the righteous, and his ears are open unto their prayers: but the face of the Lord is against them that do evil.

1 John 5:7 For there are three that bear record in heaven, the Father, the Word, and the Holy Ghost: and these three are one.

Revelation 4:11 Thou art worthy, O Lord, to receive glory and honour and power: for thou hast created all things, and for thy pleasure they are and were created.

*2 Chronicles 16:9 For the eyes of the Lord run to and fro throughout the whole earth, to shew himself strong in the behalf of them whose heart is perfect toward him.

*Amos 3:3 Can two walk together, except they be agreed?

Psalm 40:6 Sacrifice and offering thou didst not desire; mine ears hast thou opened: burnt offering and sin offering hast thou not required.7 Then said I, Lo, I come: in the volume of the book it is written of me,8 I delight to do thy will, O my God: yea, thy law is within my heart.

*Matthew 16:15 He saith unto them, But whom say ye that I am?16 And Simon Peter answered and said, Thou art the Christ, the Son of the living God.17 And Jesus answered and said unto him, Blessed art thou, Simon Barjona: for flesh and blood hath not revealed it unto thee, but my Father which is in heaven.18 And I say also unto thee, That thou art Peter, and upon this rock I will build my church; and the gates of hell shall not prevail against it.19 And I will give unto thee the keys of the kingdom of heaven: and whatsoever thou shalt bind on earth shall be bound in heaven: and whatsoever thou shalt loose on earth shall be loosed in heaven.

CHAPTER TWO
JESUS CHRIST

All of our life as a believer is based upon the revelation of **Jesus Christ**. From Matthew chapter 1 to the end of the book of Revelation, Jesus Christ is spoken of in a personal way almost 10,000 times. It is at **the revelation of Jesus Christ** in which faith will arise in your heart to accomplish the perfect will of the Father. Without this **revelation** of **who Jesus Christ really is**, we will not be to accomplish anything of eternal value. Go over these Scriptures slowly as you meditate upon them, asking the **Holy Spirit** to quicken them to you in a profound way, in order to **transform you into the likeness and the image of God**. In order to become a partaker of all of **God's** wonderful nature and divine characteristics.

The Reality of Christ

*Luke 4:18 The Spirit of the Lord is upon me, because he hath anointed me to preach the gospel to the poor; he hath sent me to heal the brokenhearted, to preach deliverance to the captives, and recovering of sight to the blind, to set at liberty them that are bruised, 19 to preach the acceptable year of the Lord.

*John 15:5 I am the vine, ye are the branches: He that abideth in me, and I in him, the same bringeth forth much fruit: for without me ye can do nothing.

*John 1:1 In the beginning was the Word, and the Word was with God, and the Word was God. 2 The same was in the beginning with God. 3 All things were made by him; and without him was not anything made that was made. 4 In him was life; and the life was the light of men. 5 And the light shineth in darkness; and the darkness comprehended it not.

*John 1:14 And the Word was made flesh, and dwelt among us, (and we beheld his glory, the glory as of the only begotten of the Father,) full of grace and truth.

*Colossians 3:1 If ye then be risen with Christ, seek those things which are above, where Christ sitteth on the right hand of God. 2 Set your affection on things above, not on things on the earth. 3 For ye are dead, and your life is hid with Christ in God. 4 When Christ, who is our life, shall appear, then shall ye also appear with him in glory.

*1 Timothy 3:16 And without controversy great is the mystery of godliness: God was manifest in the flesh, justified in the Spirit, seen of angels, preached unto the Gentiles, believed on in the world, received up into glory.

*Isaiah 9:6 For unto us a child is born, unto us a son is given: and the government shall be upon his shoulder: and his name shall be called Wonderful, Counsellor, The mighty God, The everlasting Father, The Prince of Peace.

*Acts 10:38 how God anointed Jesus of Nazareth with the Holy Ghost and with power: who went about doing good, and healing all that were oppressed of the devil; for God was with him.

*1 John 3:8 He that committeth sin is of the devil; for the devil sinneth from the beginning. For this purpose the Son of God was manifested, that he might destroy the works of the devil.

*Psalm 89:26 He shall cry unto me, Thou art my father, my God, and the rock of my salvation.27 Also I will make him my firstborn, higher than the kings of the earth.28 My mercy will I keep for him for evermore, and my covenant shall stand fast with him.29 His seed also will I make to endure forever, and his throne as the days of heaven.

---

*Hebrews 13:8 Jesus Christ the same yesterday, and today, and forever.

---

*1 Peter 3:21........ by the resurrection of Jesus Christ: 22 who is gone into heaven, and is on the right hand of God; angels and authorities and powers being made subject unto him.

---

*Isaiah 49:24 Shall the prey be taken from the mighty, or the lawful captive delivered?:25 But thus saith the Lord, Even the captives of the mighty shall be taken away, and the prey of the terrible shall be delivered: for I will contend with him that contendeth with thee, and I will save thy children.

---

*Ephesians 4: 8 wherefore he saith, When he ascended up on high, he led captivity captive, and gave gifts unto men. 9 (Now that he ascended, what is it but that he also descended first into the lower parts of the earth?10 He that descended is the same also that ascended up far above all heavens, that he might fill all things.)

---

*Colossians 1:13 who hath delivered us from the power of darkness, and hath translated us into the kingdom of his dear Son: 14 in whom we have redemption through his blood, even the forgiveness of sins: 15 who is the image of the invisible God, the firstborn of every creature: 16 for by him were all things created, that are in heaven, and that are in earth, visible and invisible, whether they be thrones, or dominions, or principalities, or powers: all things were created by him, and for him: 17 and he is before all things, and by him all things consist. 18 And he is the head of the body, the church: who is the beginning, the firstborn from the dead; that in all things he might have the preeminence. 19 For it pleased the Father that in him should all fulness dwell; 20 and, having made peace through the blood of his cross, by him to reconcile all things unto himself; by him, I say, whether they be things in earth, or things in heaven.

---

*Hebrews 2:8 thou hast put all things in subjection under his feet. For in that he put all in subjection under him, he left nothing that is not put under him. But now we see not yet all things put under him. 9 But we see Jesus, who was made a little lower than the angels for the suffering of death, crowned with glory and honour; that he by the grace of God should taste death for every man.10 For it became him, for whom are all things, and by whom are all things, in bringing many sons unto glory, to make the captain of their salvation perfect through sufferings.

---

*Acts 4:10 be it known unto you all, and to all the people of Israel, that by the name of Jesus Christ of Nazareth, whom ye crucified, whom God raised from the dead, even by him doth this man stand here before you whole. 11 This is the stone which was set at nought of you builders, which is become the head of the corner. 12 Neither is there salvation in any other: for there is none other name under heaven given among men, whereby we must be saved.

---

*Ephesians 3:14 For this cause I bow my knees unto the Father of our Lord Jesus Christ,15 of whom the whole family in heaven and earth is named, 16 that he would grant you, according to the riches of his glory, to be strengthened with might by his Spirit in the inner man; 17 that Christ may dwell in your hearts by faith; that ye, being rooted and grounded in love, 18 may be able to comprehend with all saints what is the breadth, and length, and depth, and height; 19 and to know the love of Christ, which passeth knowledge, that ye might be filled with all the fulness of God.20 Now unto him that is able to do exceeding abundantly above all that we ask or think, according to the power that worketh in us, 21 unto him be glory in the church by Christ Jesus throughout all ages, world without end. Amen.

---

* 1 Peter 1:7 That the trial of your faith, being much more

precious than of gold that perisheth, though it be tried with fire, might be found unto praise and honour and glory at the appearing of Jesus Christ:8 Whom having not seen, ye love; in whom, though now ye see him not, yet believing, ye rejoice with joy unspeakable and full of glory:9 Receiving the end of your faith, even the salvation of your souls.

In the Name of Jesus

The following scriptures are a declaration of the power and authority that we have in the **name of Jesus**. There is no other name that has been exalted above all else to bring in to subjection all of the powers and authorities that there is. As we **submit** to **Jesus Christ**, putting absolute faith and confidence in **His name** we will enter into a wonderful realm of victory. For us to be defeated, God would have to be defeated. Everything we do we do in the **name of Jesus Christ** is to be for the glory of the Father. Let us feast upon **His wonderful Name** drinking in its beauty, and eating of its substance.

*Matthew 18:20 - For where two or three are gathered together in my name, there am I in the midst of them.

*Mark 16:17 And these signs shall follow them that believe; In my name shall they cast out devils; they shall speak with new tongues;

*Luke 10:17 And the seventy returned again with joy, saying, Lord, even the devils are subject unto us through thy name.

*John 14:6 - Jesus saith unto him, I am the way, the truth, and the life: no man cometh unto the Father, but by me.

*John 10:10 - The thief cometh not, but for to steal, and to kill, and to destroy: I am come that they might have life, and that they might have [it] more abundantly.

*John 14:13-14 - And whatsoever ye shall ask in my name, that will I do, that the Father may be glorified in the Son. If ye shall ask any thing in my name, I will do [it].

*John 15:16 - Ye have not chosen me, but I have chosen you, and ordained you, that ye should go and bring forth fruit, and [that] your fruit should remain: that whatsoever ye shall ask of the Father in my name, he may give it you.

*John 16:24 - Hitherto have ye asked nothing in my name: ask, and ye shall receive, that your joy may be full.

Acts 3:6 Then Peter said, Silver and gold have I none; but such as I have give I thee: In the name of Jesus Christ of Nazareth rise up and walk.

Acts 3:16 And his name through faith in his name hath made this man strong, whom ye see and know: yea, the faith which is by him hath given him this perfect soundness in the presence of you all.

Acts 4:10 Be it known unto you all, and to all the people of Israel, that by the name of Jesus Christ of Nazareth, whom ye crucified, whom God raised from the dead, even by him doth this man stand here before you whole.

2 Corinthians 4:6 For God, who commanded the light to shine out of darkness, hath shined in our hearts, to give the light of the knowledge of the glory of God in the face of Jesus Christ.

*Romans 8:32 - He that spared not his own Son, but delivered him up for us all, how shall he not with him also freely give us all things?

2 Samuel 22:3 The God of my rock; in him will I trust: he is my shield, and the horn of my salvation, my high tower, and my refuge, my saviour; thou savest me from violence.

*Psalms 5:11 - But let all those that put their trust in thee rejoice: let them ever shout for joy, because thou defendest them: let them also that love thy name be joyful in thee.

Psalm 18:2 The Lord is my rock, and my fortress, and my deliverer; my God, my strength, in whom I will trust; my buckler, and the horn of my salvation, and my high tower.

*Proverbs 18:10 - The name of the LORD [is] a strong tower: the righteous runneth into it, and is safe.

Psalm 27:1 The Lord is my light and my salvation; whom shall I fear? the Lord is the strength of my life; of whom shall I be afraid?

*Psalm 44:5 Through thee will we push down our enemies: through thy name will we tread them under that rise up against us.

Psalm 91:2 I will say of the Lord, He is my refuge and my fortress: my God; in him will I trust.

 *Psalms 104:34 - My meditation of him shall be sweet: I will be glad in the LORD.

Psalm 144:2 My goodness, and my fortress; my high tower, and my deliverer; my shield, and he in whom I trust; who subdueth my people under me.

*Psalm 108:13 Through God we shall do valiantly: for he it is that shall tread down our enemies.

*Psalm 23 A Psalm of David.

1 The Lord is my shepherd; I shall not want.

2 He maketh me to lie down in green pastures: he leadeth me beside the still waters.

3 He restoreth my soul: he leadeth me in the paths of righteousness for his name's sake.

4 Yea, though I walk through the valley of the shadow of death, I will fear no evil: for thou art with me; thy rod and thy staff they comfort me.

5 Thou preparest a table before me in the presence of mine enemies: thou anointest my head with oil; my cup runneth over.

6 Surely goodness and mercy shall follow me all the days of my life: and I will dwell in the house of the Lord forever.

THE BLOOD OF JESUS

Matthew 20:28 Even as the Son of man came not to be ministered unto, but to minister, and to give his life a ransom for many.

Matthew 26:28 - For this is my blood of the New Testament, which is shed for many for the remission of sins.

Matthew 27:4 Saying, I have sinned in that I have betrayed the innocent blood. And they said, What is that to us? see thou to that.

Matthew 27:24 Pilate ..... saying, I am innocent of the blood of this just person: see ye to it.

Mark 14:23-24 And he took the cup, and when he had given thanks, he gave it to them: and they all drank of it. And he said unto them, This is my blood of the new testament, which is shed for many.

John 1:29 The next day John seeth Jesus coming unto him, and saith, Behold the Lamb of God, which taketh away the sin of the world.

John 19:34 But one of the soldiers with a spear pierced his side, and forthwith came there out blood and water.

John 6: 53 Then Jesus said unto them, Verily, verily, I say unto you, Except ye eat the flesh of the Son of man, and drink his blood, ye have no life in you.54 Whoso eateth my flesh, and drinketh my blood, hath eternal life; and I will raise him up at the last day.55 For my flesh is meat indeed, and my blood is drink indeed.56 He that eateth my flesh, and drinketh my blood, dwelleth in me, and I in him.57 As the living Father hath sent me, and I live by the Father: so he that eateth me, even he shall live by me.58 This is that bread which came down from heaven: not as your fathers did eat manna, and are dead: he that eateth of this bread shall live for ever..............

Acts 2:19 And I will shew wonders in heaven above, and signs in the earth beneath; blood, and fire, and vapour of smoke:

Acts 20:28 Take heed therefore unto yourselves, and to all the flock, over the which the Holy Ghost hath made you overseers, to feed the church of God, which he hath purchased with his own blood.

Romans 3:25-26 Whom God hath set forth to be a propitiation through faith in his blood, to declare his righteousness for the remission of sins that are past, through the forbearance of God; To declare, I say, at this time his righteousness: that he might be just, and the justifier of him which believeth in Jesus.

Romans 5:9 Much more then, being now justified by his blood, we shall be saved from wrath through him.

1 Corinthians 6:19 What? know ye not that your body is the temple of the Holy Ghost which is in you, which ye have of God, and ye are not your own?20 For ye are bought with a price: therefore glorify God in your body, and in your spirit, which are God's.

1 Corinthians 7:23 Ye are bought with a price; be not ye the servants of men.

1 Corinthians 10:16 The cup of blessing which we bless, is it not the communion of the blood of Christ? The bread which we break, is it not the communion of the body of Christ?

1 Corinthians 11:25 After the same manner also he took the cup, when he had supped, saying, This cup is the new testament in my blood: this do ye, as oft as ye drink it, in remembrance of me.

1 Corinthians 11:27 wherefore whosoever shall eat this bread, and drink this cup of the Lord, unworthily, shall be guilty of the body and blood of the Lord.

Ephesians 1:7 In whom we have redemption through his blood, the forgiveness of sins, according to the riches of his grace;

Ephesians 2:13 But now in Christ Jesus ye who sometimes were far off are made nigh by the blood of Christ.

Colossians 1:14 In whom we have redemption through his blood, even the forgiveness of sins:

Colossians 1:19-22 For it pleased the Father that in him should all fulness dwell; And, having made peace through the blood of his cross, by him to reconcile all things unto himself; by him, I say, whether they be things in earth, or things in heaven. And you, that were sometime alienated and enemies in your mind by wicked works, yet now hath he reconciled. In the body of his flesh through death, to present you holy and unblameable and unreproveable in his sight:

Hebrews 2:14 Forasmuch then as the children are partakers of flesh and blood, he also himself likewise took part of the same; that through death he might destroy him that had the power of death, that is, the devil;

Hebrews 9:12 - Neither by the blood of goats and calves, but by his own blood he entered in once into the holy place, having obtained eternal redemption [for us].13 For if the blood of bulls and of goats, and the ashes of an heifer sprinkling the unclean, sanctifieth to the purifying of the flesh:14 How much more shall the blood of Christ, who through the eternal Spirit offered himself without spot to God, purge your conscience from dead works to serve the living God? 15 And for this cause he is the mediator of the New Testament, that by means of death, for the redemption of the transgressions that were under the first testament, they which are called might receive the promise of eternal inheritance.

Hebrews 9:22 - And almost all things are by the law purged with blood; and without shedding of blood is no remission.

Hebrews 10:19-22Having therefore, brethren, boldness to enter into the holiest by the blood of Jesus, By a new and living way, which he hath consecrated for us, through the veil, that is to say, his flesh; And having an high priest over the house of God;Let us draw near with a true heart in full assurance of faith, having our hearts sprinkled from an evil conscience, and our bodies washed with pure water.

Hebrews 10:28-31 He that despised Moses' law died without mercy under two or three witnesses: Of how much sorer punishment, suppose ye, shall he be thought worthy, who hath trodden under foot the Son of God, and hath counted the blood of the covenant, wherewith he was sanctified, an unholy thing, and hath done despite unto the Spirit of grace? For we know him that hath said, Vengeance belongeth unto me, I will recompense, saith the Lord. And again, The Lord shall judge his people. It is a fearful thing to fall into the hands of the living God.

Hebrews 12:24 And to Jesus the mediator of the new covenant, and to the blood of sprinkling, that speaketh better things than that of Abel.

Hebrews 13:11-12 For the bodies of those beasts, whose blood is brought into the sanctuary by the high priest for sin, are burned without the camp. Wherefore Jesus also, that he might sanctify the people with his own blood, suffered without the gate.

Hebrews 13:20 - Now the God of peace, that brought again from the dead our Lord Jesus, that great shepherd of the sheep, through the blood of the everlasting covenant,

1 Peter 1:2 - Elect according to the foreknowledge of God the Father, through sanctification of the Spirit, unto obedience and sprinkling of the blood of Jesus Christ: Grace unto you, and peace, be multiplied.

1 Peter 1:18 Forasmuch as ye know that ye were not redeemed with corruptible things, as silver and gold, from your vain conversation received by tradition from your fathers;19 But with the precious blood of Christ, as of a lamb without blemish and without spot:20 Who verily was foreordained before the foundation of the world, but was manifest in these last times for you,

1 John 1:6-9 If we say that we have fellowship with him, and walk in darkness, we lie, and do not the truth: But if we walk in the light, as he is in the light, we have fellowship one with another,

and the blood of Jesus Christ his Son cleanseth us from all sin. If we say that we have no sin, we deceive ourselves, and the truth is not in us. If we confess our sins, he is faithful and just to forgive us our sins, and to cleanse us from all unrighteousness.

1 John 2:2 - And he is the propitiation for our sins: and not for ours only, but also for [the sins of] the whole world.

1 John 5:6 This is he that came by water and blood, even Jesus Christ; not by water only, but by water and blood. And it is the Spirit that beareth witness, because the Spirit is truth

Revelation 1:5-6 And from Jesus Christ, who is the faithful witness, and the first begotten of the dead, and the prince of the kings of the earth. Unto him that loved us, and washed us from our sins in his own blood, And hath made us kings and priests unto God and his Father; to him be glory and dominion for ever and ever. Amen.

Revelation 5:6 And I beheld, and, lo, in the midst of the throne and of the four beasts, and in the midst of the elders, stood a Lamb as it had been slain, having seven horns and seven eyes, which are the seven Spirits of God sent forth into all the earth.7 And he came and took the book out of the right hand of him that sat upon the throne.8 And when he had taken the book, the four beasts and four and twenty elders fell down before the Lamb, having every one of them harps, and golden vials full of odours, which are the prayers of saints.9 And they sung a new song, saying, Thou art worthy to take the book, and to open the seals thereof: for thou wast slain, and hast redeemed us to God by thy blood out of every kindred, and tongue, and people, and nation;

Revelation 7:14-17 And I said unto him, Sir, thou knowest. And he said to me, These are they which came out of great tribulation, and have washed their robes, and made them white in the blood of the Lamb. Therefore are they before the throne of God, and serve him day and night in his temple: and he that sitteth on the throne shall dwell among them. They shall hunger no more, neither thirst anymore; neither shall the sun light on them, nor any heat.

Revelation 12:10-11 And I heard a loud voice saying in heaven, Now is come salvation, and strength, and the kingdom of our God, and the power of his Christ: for the accuser of our brethren is cast down, which accused them before our God day and night. And they overcame him by the blood of the Lamb, and by the word of their testimony; and they loved not their lives unto the death.

Revelation 19:13 And he was clothed with a vesture dipped in blood: and his name is called The Word of God.

Genesis 4:10 And he said, What hast thou done? the voice of thy brother's blood crieth unto me from the ground.

Exodus 12:13 - And the blood shall be to you for a token upon the houses where ye [are]: and when I see the blood, I will pass over you, and the plague shall not be upon you to destroy [you], when I smite the land of Egypt.

Leviticus 17:11 For the life of the flesh is in the blood: and I have given it to you upon the altar to make an atonement for your souls: for it is the blood that maketh an atonement for the soul.

Ezekiel 16:6 - And when I passed by thee, and saw thee polluted in thine own blood, I said unto thee [when thou wast] in thy blood, Live; yea, I said unto thee [when thou wast] in thy blood, Live.

CHAPTER THREE
The Nature of Christ

The whole purpose of **Christ** coming was in order to bring change to our nature. When you invite Christ into your heart, the incorruptible seed of the word of life is implanted within the soil of your being. As you meditate upon the truths of this amazing plan the fruits of **Christ** will begin to be manifested in your attitude, character and nature. We must meditate upon the Scriptures in order for the Holy Spirit has that which is necessary to bring to pass the perfect will of the father into our personalities and character. The Scripture very boldly declares that we are the **sons of God**, and it does not yet appear what we shall be. That natural eyes have not seen nor ears have heard, neither entered into the heart of man what God has planned for them that love him.

*1 John 3:1 Behold, what manner of love the Father hath bestowed upon us, that we should be called the sons of God: therefore the world knoweth us not, because it knew him not. 2 Beloved, now are we the sons of God, and it doth not yet appear what we shall be: but we know that, when he shall appear, we shall be like him; for we shall see him as he is. 3 And every man that hath this hope in him purifieth himself, even as he is pure.

*2 Corinthians 5:17 Therefore if any man be in Christ, he is a new creature: old things are passed away; behold, all things are become new.

*Ezekiel 36:26 A new heart also will I give you, and a new spirit will I put within you: and I will take away the stony heart out of your flesh, and I will give you an heart of flesh.

*John 3:3 Jesus answered and said unto him, Verily, verily, I say unto thee, Except a man be born again, he cannot see the kingdom of God.

*Ephesians 4:22 That ye put off concerning the former conversation the old man, which is corrupt according to the deceitful lusts;23 And be renewed in the spirit of your mind;24 And that ye put on the new man, which after God is created in righteousness and true holiness.

*2 Corinthians 5:21 For he hath made him to be sin for us, who knew no sin; that we might be made the righteousness of God in him.

*Romans 6:5 For if we have been planted together in the likeness of his death, we shall be also in the likeness of his resurrection: 2 Corinthians 4:10 Always bearing about in the body the dying of the Lord Jesus, that the life also of Jesus might be made manifest in our body.

Colossians 2:12 Buried with him in baptism, wherein also ye are risen with him through the faith of the operation of God, who hath raised him from the dead.

Ephesians 2:5 Even when we were dead in sins, hath quickened us together with Christ, (by grace ye are saved;)6 And hath raised us up together, and made us sit together in heavenly places in Christ Jesus:

Romans 6:8 Now if we be dead with Christ, we believe that we shall also live with him:9 Knowing that Christ being raised from the dead dieth no more; death hath no more dominion over him.10 For in that he died, he died unto sin once: but in that he liveth, he liveth unto God.11 Likewise reckon ye also yourselves to be dead indeed unto sin, but alive unto God through Jesus Christ our Lord.12 Let not sin therefore reign in your mortal body, that ye should obey it in the lusts thereof.

John 12:24 Verily, verily, I say unto you, Except a corn of wheat fall into the ground and die, it abideth alone: but if it die, it bringeth forth much fruit.

---

*2 Corinthians 6:.......as God hath said, I will dwell in them, and walk in them; and I will be their God, and they shall be my people.

---

*2 Corinthians 3:18 But we all, with open face beholding as in a glass the glory of the Lord, are changed into the same image from glory to glory, even as by the Spirit of the Lord.

---

*2 Peter 1: 2 Grace and peace be multiplied unto you through the knowledge of God, and of Jesus our Lord,3 According as his divine power hath given unto us all things that pertain unto life and godliness, through the knowledge of him that hath called us to glory and virtue:4 Whereby are given unto us exceeding great and precious promises: that by these ye might be partakers of the divine nature, having escaped the corruption that is in the world through lust.5 And beside this, giving all diligence, add to your faith virtue; and to virtue knowledge;6 And to knowledge temperance; and to temperance patience; and to patience godliness;7 And to godliness brotherly kindness; and to brotherly kindness charity.8 For if these things be in you, and abound, they make you that ye shall neither be barren nor unfruitful in the knowledge of our Lord Jesus Christ.

---

*Romans 8: 12 Therefore, brethren, we are debtors, not to the flesh, to live after the flesh.13 For if ye live after the flesh, ye shall die: but if ye through the Spirit do mortify the deeds of the body, ye shall live.14 For as many as are led by the Spirit of God, they are the sons of God.15 For ye have not received the spirit of bondage again to fear; but ye have received the Spirit of adoption, whereby we cry, Abba, Father.

*Romans 8: 17 Now the Lord is that Spirit: and where the Spirit of the Lord is, there is liberty. 18 For I reckon that the sufferings of this present time are not worthy to be compared with the glory which shall be revealed in us.

*Galatians 4:6 And because ye are sons, God hath sent forth the Spirit of his Son into your hearts, crying, Abba, Father.

*1 John 4:4 Ye are of God, little children, and have overcome them: because greater is he that is in you, than he that is in the world.

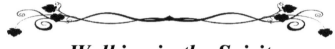

Walking in the Spirit

In order to walk in the spirit we must be full of the word of God. The divine influence of the Holy Spirit must have complete possession of our lives. There are many scriptures that deal with his particular subject of living, moving, operating, and flowing in the Holy Ghost. God is looking for those who will be completely yielded and surrendered to Christ in all areas of their life. When we walk in the spirit we will not fulfill the lust of the flesh. Meditate upon these realities and you will soon begin to see wonderful and amazing transformation in all that you do and say. When you walk in the spirit the fruits of the spirit will be manifested in your life.

*Galatians 5:16 This I say then, Walk in the Spirit, and ye shall not fulfil the lust of the flesh. 17 For the flesh lusteth against the Spirit, and the Spirit against the flesh: and these are contrary the one to the other: so that ye cannot do the things that ye would.

*Galatians 5:24 And they that are Christ's have crucified the flesh with the affections and lusts. 25 If we live in the Spirit, let us also walk in the Spirit. 26 Let us not be desirous of vain glory, provoking one another, envying one another.

*1 Peter 2:11 Dearly beloved, I beseech you as strangers and pilgrims, abstain from fleshly lusts, which war against the soul;

*Colossians 3:9 Lie not one to another, seeing that ye have put off the old man with his deeds;10 And have put on the new man, which is renewed in knowledge after the image of him that created him:

*Deuteronomy8:6 Therefore thou shalt keep the commandments of the Lord thy God, to walk in his ways, and to fear him.

*Romans 8:1 There is therefore now no condemnation to them which are in Christ Jesus, who walk not after the flesh, but after the Spirit. 2 For the law of the Spirit of life in Christ Jesus hath made me free from the law of sin and death. 3 For what the law could not do, in that it was weak through the flesh, God sending his own Son in the likeness of sinful flesh, and for sin, condemned sin in the flesh:

*Colossians 1:10 that ye might walk worthy of the Lord unto all pleasing, being fruitful in every good work, and increasing in the knowledge of God;

*1 Thessalonians 2:12 that ye would walk worthy of God, who hath called you unto his kingdom and glory.

*2 Corinthians 5:7 (for we walk by faith, not by sight)

Romans 1:17 For therein is the righteousness of God revealed from faith to faith: as it is written, The just shall live by faith.

*Galatians 2:20 I am crucified with Christ: nevertheless I live; yet not I, but Christ liveth in me: and the life which I now live in the flesh I live by the faith of the Son of God, who loved me, and gave himself for me.

*Galatians 3:11 But that no man is justified by the law in the sight of God, it is evident: for, The just shall live by faith.

*Hebrews 10:38 Now the just shall live by faith: but if any man draw back, my soul shall have no pleasure in him.

*John 8:12 Then spake Jesus again unto them, saying, I am the light of the world: he that followeth me shall not walk in darkness, but shall have the light of life.

*Ephesians 5:8 For ye were sometimes darkness, but now are ye light in the Lord: walk as children of light:

*1 John 1:7 But if we walk in the light, as he is in the light, we have fellowship one with another, and the blood of Jesus Christ his Son cleanseth us from all sin.

The Fruits of Christ

*Galatians 5:22 But the fruit of the Spirit is love, joy, peace, longsuffering, gentleness, goodness, faith, 23 meekness, temperance: against such there is no law.

*Colossians 3:12 Put on therefore, as the elect of God, holy and beloved, bowels of mercies, kindness, humbleness of mind, meekness, longsuffering;13 Forbearing one another, and forgiving one another, if any man have a quarrel against any: even as Christ forgave you, so also do ye.14 And above all these things put on charity, which is the bond of perfectness.15 And let the peace of God rule in your hearts, to the which also ye are called in one body; and be ye thankful.

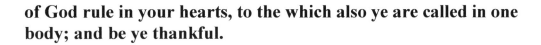

    *Ephesians 5:9 (For the fruit of the Spirit is in all goodness and righteousness and truth;)

    *John 15:2 Every branch in me that beareth not fruit he taketh away: and every branch that beareth fruit, he purgeth it, that it may bring forth more fruit.

    *James 3:17 But the wisdom that is from above is first pure, then peaceable, gentle, and easy to be intreated, full of mercy and good fruits, without partiality, and without hypocrisy.18 And the fruit of righteousness is sown in peace of them that make peace.

    *Philippians 4:4 Rejoice in the Lord always: and again I say, Rejoice.5 Let your moderation be known unto all men. The Lord is at hand.6 Be careful for nothing; but in every thing by prayer and supplication with thanksgiving let your requests be made known unto God.7 And the peace of God, which passeth all understanding, shall keep your hearts and minds through Christ Jesus.

    *2 Peter 1:5 And beside this, giving all diligence, add to your faith virtue; and to virtue knowledge;6 And to knowledge temperance; and to temperance patience; and to patience godliness;7 And to godliness brotherly kindness; and to brotherly kindness charity.8 For if these things be in you, and abound, they make you that ye shall neither be barren nor unfruitful in the knowledge of our Lord Jesus Christ.

*Colossians 1:10 That ye might walk worthy of the Lord unto all pleasing, being fruitful in every good work, and increasing in the knowledge of God;

God's Love For Us in Christ

Romans 4:25 Who was delivered for our offences, and was raised again for our justification.

* Romans 5:6 For when we were yet without strength, in due time Christ died for the ungodly.

*John 3:16 - For God so loved the world, that he gave his only begotten Son, that whosoever believeth in him should not perish, but have everlasting life.

*1 John 4:18 - There is no fear in love; but perfect love casteth out fear: because fear hath torment. He that feareth is not made perfect in love.

*John 15:13 - Greater love hath no man than this, that a man lay down his life for his friends.

*1 John 4:10 - Herein is love, not that we loved God, but that he loved us, and sent his Son [to be] the propitiation for our sins.

*John 14:21 - He that hath my commandments, and keepeth them, he it is that loveth me: and he that loveth me shall be loved of my Father, and I will love him, and will manifest myself to him.

1 John 3:16 Hereby perceive we the love of God, because he laid down his life for us: and we ought to lay down our lives for the brethren.

*1 John 4:7 - Beloved, let us love one another: for love is of God; and every one that loveth is born of God, and knoweth God.

1 John 4:9 In this was manifested the love of God toward us, because that God sent his only begotten Son into the world, that we might live through him.10 Herein is love, not that we loved God, but that he loved us, and sent his Son to be the propitiation for our sins.

2 Corinthians 5:19 To wit, that God was in Christ, reconciling the world unto himself, not imputing their trespasses unto them; and hath committed unto us the word of reconciliation.20 Now then we are ambassadors for Christ, as though God did beseech you by us: we pray you in Christ's stead, be ye reconciled to God.21 For he hath made him to be sin for us, who knew no sin; that we might be made the righteousness of God in him.

Romans 5:8 But God commendeth his love toward us, in that, while we were yet sinners, Christ died for us.9 Much more then, being now justified by his blood, we shall be saved from wrath through him.10 For if, when we were enemies, we were reconciled to God by the death of his Son, much more, being reconciled, we shall be saved by his life.

Ephesians 2:4 But God, who is rich in mercy, for his great love wherewith he loved us,5 Even when we were dead in sins, hath quickened us together with Christ, (by grace ye are saved;)

1 Peter 2:24 Who his own self bare our sins in his own body on the tree, that we, being dead to sins, should live unto righteousness: by whose stripes ye were healed.

1 Peter 3:18 For Christ also hath once suffered for sins, the just for the unjust, that he might bring us to God, being put to death in the flesh, but quickened by the Spirit:

1 John 4:19 We love him, because he first loved us.

Isaiah 53:6 All we like sheep have gone astray; we have turned every one to his own way; and the Lord hath laid on him the iniquity of us all.

Joy In Christ

*Philippians 4:4 - Rejoice in the Lord alway: [and] again I say, Rejoice.

*1 Peter 1:8 - Whom having not seen, ye love; in whom, though now ye see [him] not, yet believing, ye rejoice with joy unspeakable and full of glory:

*John 16:24 - Hitherto have ye asked nothing in my name: ask, and ye shall receive, that your joy may be full.

*Romans 15:13 - Now the God of hope fill you with all joy and peace in believing, that ye may abound in hope, through the power of the Holy Ghost.

*Romans 14:17 - For the kingdom of God is not meat and drink; but righteousness, and peace, and joy in the Holy Ghost.

*Romans 5:11 - And not only [so], but we also joy in God through our Lord Jesus Christ, by whom we have now received the atonement.

*1 Peter 4:13 - But rejoice, inasmuch as ye are partakers of Christ's sufferings; that, when his glory shall be revealed, ye may be glad also with exceeding joy.

*Colossians 1:11 - Strengthened with all might, according to his glorious power, unto all patience and longsuffering with joyfulness;

*Isaiah 55:12 - For ye shall go out with joy, and be led forth with peace: the mountains and the hills shall break forth before you into singing, and all the trees of the field shall clap [their] hands.

*Proverbs 17:22 - A merry heart doeth good [like] a medicine: but a broken spirit drieth the bones.

*Philippians 3:3 - For we are the circumcision, which worship God in the spirit, and rejoice in Christ Jesus, and have no confidence in the flesh.

*Psalms 70:4 - Let all those that seek thee rejoice and be glad in thee: and let such as love thy salvation say continually, Let God be magnified.

*Psalms 104:34 - My meditation of him shall be sweet: I will be glad in the LORD.

*Psalms 100:2 - Serve the LORD with gladness: come before his presence with singing.

*Psalms 64:10 - The righteous shall be glad in the LORD, and shall trust in him; and all the upright in heart shall glory.

*Psalms 30:11 - Thou hast turned for me my mourning into dancing: thou hast put off my sackcloth, and girded me with gladness;

*Psalms 19:8 - The statutes of the LORD [are] right, rejoicing the heart: the commandment of the LORD [is] pure, enlightening the eyes.

---

*Psalms 16:11 - Thou wilt shew me the path of life: in thy presence [is] fulness of joy; at thy right hand [there are] pleasures for evermore.

---

*Psalms 5:11 - But let all those that put their trust in thee rejoice: let them ever shout for joy, because thou defendest them: let them also that love thy name be joyful in thee.

---

*1 Thessalonians 2:19 - For what [is] our hope, or joy, or crown of rejoicing? [Are] not even ye in the presence of our Lord Jesus Christ at his coming?

CHAPTER FOUR
CONTINUED FRUITS

<u>*Peace In Christ*</u>

*Matthew 5:9 - Blessed [are] the peacemakers: for they shall be called the children of God.

*Philippians 4:7 - And the peace of God, which passeth all understanding, shall keep your hearts and minds through Christ Jesus.

*2 Thessalonians 3:16 - Now the Lord of peace himself give you peace always by all means. The Lord [be] with you all.

*John 14:27 - Peace I leave with you, my peace I give unto you: not as the world giveth, give I unto you. Let not your heart be troubled, neither let it be afraid.

*1 Peter 3:11 - Let him eschew evil, and do good; let him seek peace, and ensue it.

*1 Peter 5:7 - Casting all your care upon him; for he careth for you.

*Isaiah 26:3 - Thou wilt keep [him] in perfect peace, [whose] mind [is] stayed [on thee]: because he trusteth in thee.

*John 16:33 - These things I have spoken unto you, that in me ye might have peace. In the world ye shall have tribulation: but be of good cheer; I have overcome the world.

*Hebrews 12:14 - Follow peace with all [men], and holiness, without which no man shall see the Lord:

*Philippians 4:9 - Those things, which ye have both learned, and received, and heard, and seen in me, do: and the God of peace shall be with you.

*Isaiah 12:2 - Behold, God [is] my salvation; I will trust, and not be afraid: for the LORD JEHOVAH [is] my strength and [my] song; he also is become my salvation.

*Romans 8:6 - For to be carnally minded [is] death; but to be spiritually minded [is] life and peace.

*Colossians 3:15 - And let the peace of God rule in your hearts, to the which also ye are called in one body; and be ye thankful.

*James 3:18 - And the fruit of righteousness is sown in peace of them that make peace.

*Romans 14:19 - Let us therefore follow after the things which make for peace, and things wherewith one may edify another.

*Psalms 37:4 - Delight thyself also in the LORD; and he shall give thee the desires of thine heart.

*Isaiah 32:17 - And the work of righteousness shall be peace; and the effect of righteousness quietness and assurance for ever.

*Proverbs 3:24 - When thou liest down, thou shalt not be afraid: yea, thou shalt lie down, and thy sleep shall be sweet.

*John 7:38 - He that believeth on me, as the scripture hath said, out of his belly shall flow rivers of living water.

*Isaiah 54:13 - And all thy children [shall be] taught of the LORD; and great [shall be] the peace of thy children.

*Psalms 34:14 - Depart from evil, and do good; seek peace, and pursue it.

*1 Peter 3:10 - For he that will love life, and see good days, let him refrain his tongue from evil, and his lips that they speak no guile:

*Jeremiah 33:6 - Behold, I will bring it health and cure, and I will cure them, and will reveal unto them the abundance of peace and truth.

*Isaiah 55:12 - For ye shall go out with joy, and be led forth with peace: the mountains and the hills shall break forth before you into singing, and all the trees of the field shall clap [their] hands.

Longsuffering Of Chist

*Ephesians 4:2 - With all lowliness and meekness, with longsuffering, forbearing one another in love;

*2 Peter 3:9 - The Lord is not slack concerning his promise, as some men count slackness; but is longsuffering to us-ward, not willing that any should perish, but that all should come to repentance.

---

*Romans 8:28 - And we know that all things work together for good to them that love God, to them who are the called according to [his] purpose.

---

2 Peter 3:15 And account that the longsuffering of our Lord is salvation; even as our beloved brother Paul also according to the wisdom given unto him hath written unto you;

Luke 13:8 And he answering said unto him, Lord, let it alone this year also, till I shall dig about it, and dung it:

Joel 2:13 And rend your heart, and not your garments, and turn unto the Lord your God: for he is gracious and merciful, slow to anger, and of great kindness, and repenteth him of the evil.

Romans 3:25 Whom God hath set forth to be a propitiation through faith in his blood, to declare his righteousness for the remission of sins that are past, through the forbearance of God;

Isaiah 30:18 And therefore will the Lord wait, that he may be gracious unto you, and therefore will he be exalted, that he may have mercy upon you: for the Lord is a God of judgment: blessed are all they that wait for him.

Ezekiel 20:17 Nevertheless mine eye spared them from destroying them, neither did I make an end of them in the wilderness.

---

1 Peter 3:20 Which sometime were disobedient, when once the longsuffering of God waited in the days of Noah, while the ark

was a preparing, wherein few, that is, eight souls were saved by water.

Numbers 14:18 The Lord is longsuffering, and of great mercy, forgiving iniquity and transgression, and by no means clearing the guilty, visiting the iniquity of the fathers upon the children unto the third and fourth generation.

Psalm 86:15 But thou, O Lord, art a God full of compassion, and gracious, long suffering, and plenteous in mercy and truth.

---

*Ezekiel 18:20 - The soul that sinneth, it shall die. The son shall not bear the iniquity of the father, neither shall the father bear the iniquity of the son.

---

*Ezekiel 18:4 - Behold, all souls are mine; as the soul of the father, so also the soul of the son is mine: the soul that sinneth, it shall die.

---

*Exodus 34:6 - And the LORD passed by before him, and proclaimed, The LORD, The LORD God, merciful and gracious, longsuffering, and abundant in goodness and truth,

---

*Romans 2:4 - Or despisest thou the riches of his goodness and forbearance and longsuffering; not knowing that the goodness of God leadeth thee to repentance?

Gentleness Of Christ

Matthew 11:29 Take my yoke upon you, and learn of me; for I am meek and lowly in heart: and ye shall find rest unto your souls.

Matthew 21:5 Tell ye the daughter of Sion, Behold, thy King cometh unto thee, meek, and sitting upon an ass, and a colt the foal of an ass.

John 14:21 He that hath my commandments, and keepeth them, he it is that loveth me: and he that loveth me shall be loved of my Father, and I will love him, and will manifest myself to him......23 Jesus answered and said unto him, If a man love me, he will keep my words: and my Father will love him, and we will come unto him, and make our abode with him.24 He that loveth me not keepeth not my sayings: and the word which ye hear is not mine, but the Father's which sent me.

John 15:10 If ye keep my commandments, ye shall abide in my love; even as I have kept my Father's commandments, and abide in his love.11 These things have I spoken unto you, that my joy might remain in you, and that your joy might be full.12 This is my commandment, That ye love one another, as I have loved you.13 Greater love hath no man than this, that a man lay down his life for his friends.14 Ye are my friends, if ye do whatsoever I command you.

---

2 Corinthians 10:10 Now I Paul my self-beseech you by the meekness and gentleness of Christ, who in presence am base among you, but being absent am bold toward you:

Colossians 3:12 Put on therefore, as the elect of God, holy and beloved, bowels of mercies, kindness, humbleness of mind, meekness, longsuffering;13 Forbearing one another, and forgiving one another, if any man have a quarrel against any: even as Christ forgave you, so also do ye.

---

1 Timothy 6:11 But thou, O man of God, flee these things; and follow after righteousness, godliness, faith, love, patience, meekness.

1 Peter 2:21 For even hereunto were ye called: because Christ also suffered for us, leaving us an example, that ye should follow his steps:22 Who did no sin, neither was guile found in his mouth:23 Who, when he was reviled, reviled not again; when he suffered, he threatened not; but committed himself to him that judgeth righteously:

Zechariah 9:9 Rejoice greatly, O daughter of Zion; shout, O daughter of Jerusalem: behold, thy King cometh unto thee: he is just, and having salvation; lowly, and riding upon an ass, and upon a colt the foal of an ass.

Hebrews 5:9 And being made perfect, he became the author of eternal salvation unto all them that obey him;*1 Peter 2:23 - Who, when he was reviled, reviled not again; when he suffered, he threatened not; but committed [himself] to him that judgeth righteously:

---

*Isaiah 40:11 - He shall feed his flock like a shepherd: he shall gather the lambs with his arm, and carry [them] in his bosom, [and] shall gently lead those that are with young.

---

*Isaiah 53:7 - He was oppressed, and he was afflicted, yet he opened not his mouth: he is brought as a lamb to the slaughter, and as a sheep before her shearers is dumb, so he openeth not his mouth.

---

*Psalms 18:35 - Thou hast also given me the shield of thy salvation: and thy right hand hath holden me up, and thy gentleness hath made me great.

---

*2 Timothy 2:24-26 - And the servant of the Lord must not strive; but be gentle unto all [men], apt to teach, patient,   (Read More...)

---

*James 1:19-20 - Wherefore, my beloved brethren, let every man be swift to hear, slow to speak, slow to wrath: (Read More...)

---

*Colossians 3:12 - Put on therefore, as the elect of God, holy and beloved, bowels of mercies, kindness, humbleness of mind, meekness, longsuffering;

---

*Proverbs 15:1 - A soft answer turneth away wrath: but grievous words stir up anger.

---

*Micah 6:8 - He hath shewed thee, O man, what [is] good; and what doth the LORD require of thee, but to do justly, and to love mercy, and to walk humbly with thy God?

---

*Matthew 6:19-21 - Lay not up for yourselves treasures upon earth, where moth and rust doth corrupt, and where thieves break through and steal: (Read More...)

---

*Hebrews 13:5 - [Let your] conversation [be] without covetousness; [and be] content with such things as ye have: for he hath said, I will never leave thee, nor forsake thee.

---

*1 Timothy 6:11 - But thou, O man of God, flee these things; and follow after righteousness, godliness, faith, love, patience, meekness.

Goodness Of Christ

Mark 10:18 And Jesus said unto him, Why callest thou me good? there is none good but one, that is, God.

John 10:11 I am the good shepherd: the good shepherd giveth his life for the sheep.

John 10:14 I am the good shepherd, and know my sheep, and am known of mine.

Acts 10:38 How God anointed Jesus of Nazareth with the Holy Ghost and with power: who went about doing good, and healing all that were oppressed of the devil; for God was with him.

Romans 2:4 Or despisest thou the riches of his goodness and forbearance and longsuffering; not knowing that the goodness of God leadeth thee to repentance?

Psalm 145:9 The Lord is good to all: and his tender mercies are over all his works.

Matthew 12:35 A good man out of the good treasure of the heart bringeth forth good things: and an evil man out of the evil treasure bringeth forth evil things.

Romans 11:22 Behold therefore the goodness and severity of God: on them which fell, severity; but toward thee, goodness, if thou continue in his goodness: otherwise thou also shalt be cut off.

Romans 12:21 Be not overcome of evil, but overcome evil with good.

Galatians 5:22 But the fruit of the Spirit is love, joy, peace, longsuffering, gentleness, goodness, faith,23 Meekness, temperance: against such there is no law.24 And they that are Christ's have crucified the flesh with the affections and lusts.

Ephesians 1:5 Having predestinated us unto the adoption of children by Jesus Christ to himself, according to the good pleasure of his will,

Ephesians 1:9 Having made known unto us the mystery of his will, according to his good pleasure which he hath purposed in himself:

Philippians 1:6 Being confident of this very thing, that he which hath begun a good work in you will perform it until the day of Jesus Christ:

Philippians 2:13 For it is God which worketh in you both to will and to do of his good pleasure.

2 Thessalonians 2:16 Now our Lord Jesus Christ himself, and God, even our Father, which hath loved us, and hath given us everlasting consolation and good hope through grace,:17 Comfort your hearts, and stablish you in every good word and work.

Hebrews 13:21 Make you perfect in every good work to do his will, working in you that which is wellpleasing in his sight, through Jesus Christ; to whom be glory for ever and ever. Amen.

James 1:17 Every good gift and every perfect gift is from above, and cometh down from the Father of lights, with whom is no variableness, neither shadow of turning.

3 John 1:11 Beloved, follow not that which is evil, but that which is good. He that doeth good is of God: but he that doeth evil hath not seen God.

*Romans 8:28 - And we know that all things work together for good to them that love God, to them who are the called according to [his] purpose.

*Psalms 31:19 - [Oh] how great [is] thy goodness, which thou hast laid up for them that fear thee; [which] thou hast wrought for them that trust in thee before the sons of men!

*Psalms 23:6 - Surely goodness and mercy shall follow me all the days of my life: and I will dwell in the house of the LORD for ever.

*Romans 12:9 ..... Abhor that which is evil; cleave to that which is good.

Faithfulness Of Christ

Revelation 1:5 And from Jesus Christ, who is the faithful witness, and the first begotten of the dead, and the prince of the kings of the earth. Unto him that loved us, and washed us from our sins in his own blood,

Revelation 3:14 These things saith the Amen, the faithful and true witness, the beginning of the creation of God;

Revelation 19:11 And I saw heaven opened, and behold a white horse; and he that sat upon him was called Faithful and True, and in righteousness he doth judge and make war.

1 Corinthians 1:9 God is faithful, by whom ye were called unto the fellowship of his Son Jesus Christ our Lord.

1 Thessalonians 5:24Faithful is he that calleth you, who also will do it.

2 Thessalonians 3:3 But the Lord is faithful, who shall stablish you, and keep you from evil.

1 Timothy 1:15 This is a faithful saying, and worthy of all acceptation, that Christ Jesus came into the world to save sinners; of whom I am chief.

2 Timothy 2:11 It is a faithful saying: For if we be dead with him, we shall also live with him:

Hebrews 2:17 Wherefore in all things it behoved him to be made like unto his brethren, that he might be a merciful and faithful high priest in things pertaining to God, to make reconciliation for the sins of the people.

Hebrews 3:2 Who was faithful to him that appointed him, as also Moses was faithful in all his house.

Hebrews 10:23 Let us hold fast the profession of our faith without wavering; (for he is faithful that promised;)

1 Peter 4:19 Wherefore let them that suffer according to the will of God commit the keeping of their souls to him in well doing, as unto a faithful Creator.*Proverbs 28:20 - A faithful man shall abound with blessings: but he that maketh haste to be rich shall not be innocent.

*Luke 16:10-12 - He that is faithful in that which is least is faithful also in much: and he that is unjust in the least is unjust also in much.

*John 14:15 - If ye love me, keep my commandments.

*Jeremiah 1:5 - Before I formed thee in the belly I knew thee; and before thou camest forth out of the womb I sanctified thee, [and] I ordained thee a prophet unto the nations.

*1 Corinthians 10:13 - There hath no temptation taken you but such as is common to man: but God [is] faithful, who will not suffer you to be tempted above that ye are able; but will with the temptation also make a way to escape, that ye may be able to bear [it].

*Matthew 10:22 - And ye shall be hated of all [men] for my name's sake: but he that endureth to the end shall be saved.

*Psalms 91:4 - He shall cover thee with his feathers, and under his wings shalt thou trust: his truth [shall be thy] shield and buckler.

*2 Peter 3:9 - The Lord is not slack concerning his promise, as some men count slackness; but is longsuffering to us-ward, not willing that any should perish, but that all should come to repentance.

*Romans 10:9 - That if thou shalt confess with thy mouth the Lord Jesus, and shalt believe in thine heart that God hath raised him from the dead, thou shalt be saved.

*Proverbs 25:19 Confidence in an unfaithful man in time of trouble is like a broken tooth, and a foot out of joint.

Meekness Of Christ

*Matthew 5:5 - Blessed [are] the meek: for they shall inherit the earth.

*Matthew 11:29 - Take my yoke upon you, and learn of me; for I am meek and lowly in heart: and ye shall find rest unto your souls.

---

*Psalms 25:9 - The meek will he guide in judgment: and the meek will he teach his way.

---

*1 Peter 3:4 - But [let it be] the hidden man of the heart, in that which is not corruptible, [even the ornament] of a meek and quiet spirit, which is in the sight of God of great price.

---

*Psalms 37:11 - But the meek shall inherit the earth; and shall delight themselves in the abundance of peace.

---

*James 3:13 - Who [is] a wise man and endued with knowledge among you? let him shew out of a good conversation his works with meekness of wisdom.

---

*Numbers 12:3 - (Now the man Moses [was] very meek, above all the men which [were] upon the face of the earth.)

---

*James 1:21 - Wherefore lay apart all filthiness and superfluity of naughtiness, and receive with meekness the engrafted word, which is able to save your souls.

---

*Galatians 6:1 - Brethren, if a man be overtaken in a fault, ye which are spiritual, restore such an one in the spirit of meekness; considering thyself, lest thou also be tempted.

---

*Ephesians 4:2 - With all lowliness and meekness, with longsuffering, forbearing one another in love;

---

*1 Peter 5:7 - Casting all your care upon him; for he careth for you.

*2 Timothy 2:25 - In meekness instructing those that oppose themselves; if God peradventure will give them repentance to the acknowledging of the truth;

*1 Timothy 6:11 - But thou, O man of God, flee these things; and follow after righteousness, godliness, faith, love, patience, meekness.

*Psalms 22:26 - The meek shall eat and be satisfied: they shall praise the LORD that seek him: your heart shall live for ever.

*Romans 12:18 - If it be possible, as much as lieth in you, live peaceably with all men.

*Matthew 16:24 - Then said Jesus unto his disciples, If any [man] will come after me, let him deny himself, and take up his cross, and follow me.

*Matthew 5:9 - Blessed [are] the peacemakers: for they shall be called the children of God.

Temperance Of Christ

Hebrews 4:15 For we have not an high priest which cannot be touched with the feeling of our infirmities; but was in all points tempted like as we are, yet without sin.

Hebrews 2:17 Wherefore in all things it behoved him to be made like unto his brethren, that he might be a merciful and faithful high priest in things pertaining to God, to make reconciliation for the sins of the people.18 For in that he himself hath suffered being tempted, he is able to succour them that are tempted.

Hebrews 7:26 For such an high priest became us, who is holy, harmless, undefiled, separate from sinners, and made higher than the heavens;

1 John 3:5 And ye know that he was manifested to take away our sins; and in him is no sin.

1 Peter 2:22 Who did no sin, neither was guile found in his mouth:*1 Corinthians 9:27 - But I keep under my body, and bring [it] into subjection: lest that by any means, when I have preached to others, I myself should be a castaway.

*Romans 13:14 - But put ye on the Lord Jesus Christ, and make not provision for the flesh, to [fulfil] the lusts [thereof].

*2 Peter 1:6 - And to knowledge temperance; and to temperance patience; and to patience godliness;

*1 Peter 5:8 - Be sober, be vigilant; because your adversary the devil, as a roaring lion, walketh about, seeking whom he may devour:

*1 Thessalonians 5:21 - Prove all things; hold fast that which is good.

*Galatians 6:7-8 - Be not deceived; God is not mocked: for whatsoever a man soweth, that shall he also reap.   (Read More...)

*Romans 8:37 - Nay, in all these things we are more than conquerors through him that loved us.

*John 11:25 - Jesus said unto her, I am the resurrection, and the life: he that believeth in me, though he were dead, yet shall he live:

---

*Philippians 4:13 - I can do all things through Christ which strengtheneth me.

---

*2 Corinthians 5:21 - For he hath made him [to be] sin for us, who knew no sin; that we might be made the righteousness of God in him.

---

*Romans 3:23 - For all have sinned, and come short of the glory of God;

---

*John 8:32 - And ye shall know the truth, and the truth shall make you free.

---

*John 14:6 - Jesus saith unto him, I am the way, the truth, and the life: no man cometh unto the Father, but by me.

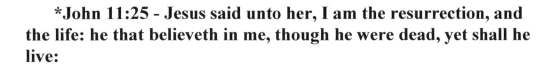

The Revelation of Christ

Romans 16:25 Now to him that is of power to stablish you according to my gospel, and the preaching of Jesus Christ, according to the revelation of the mystery, which was kept secret since the world began,

---

Galatians 1:12 For I neither received it of man, neither was I taught it, but by the revelation of Jesus Christ.

Ephesians 1:17 That the God of our Lord Jesus Christ, the Father of glory, may give unto you the spirit of wisdom and revelation in the knowledge of him:

Ephesians 3:9 And to make all men see what is the fellowship of the mystery, which from the beginning of the world hath been hid in God, who created all things by Jesus Christ:

1 Peter 1:13 Wherefore gird up the loins of your mind, be sober, and hope to the end for the grace that is to be brought unto you at the revelation of Jesus Christ;

2 Peter 1:2 Grace and peace be multiplied unto you through the knowledge of God, and of Jesus our Lord,

Revelation 1:1 The Revelation of Jesus Christ, which God gave unto him, to shew unto his servants things which must shortly come to pass; and he sent and signified it by his angel unto his servant John:

CHAPTER FIVE
HEALING IN CHRIST

Healing is such an important part of God's redemptive plan for men provided through **Christ**. There's many Scriptures that are given to us in the old and the new pertaining to this particular subject. As you hide the word of God in your heart through meditation may the Scriptures become alive on the inside of you. May the Lord grant unto you a revelation of the price that was paid for your physical, mental, and emotional healing. For 40 years I have fought the fight of faith when it comes to divine healing for myself and many others. **Christ** has paid the ultimate price for my physical healing, and I will not allow the enemy to rob me of it. I hope you will be of the same mindset.

*Isa 53:1 Who hath believed our report? and to whom is the arm of the Lord revealed?2 For he shall grow up before him as a tender plant, and as a root out of a dry ground: he hath no form nor comeliness; and when we shall see him, there is no beauty that we should desire him.3 He is despised and rejected of men; a man of sorrows, and acquainted with grief: and we hid as it were our faces from him; he was despised, and we esteemed him not.4 Surely he hath borne our griefs, and carried our sorrows: yet we did esteem him stricken, smitten of God, and afflicted.5 But he was wounded for our transgressions, he was bruised for our iniquities: the chastisement of our peace was upon him; and with his stripes we are healed.6 All we like sheep have gone astray; we have turned every one to his own way; and the Lord hath laid on him the iniquity of us all.7 He was oppressed, and he was afflicted, yet he opened not his mouth: he is brought as a lamb to the slaughter, and as a sheep before her shearers is dumb, so he openeth not his mouth.8 He was taken from prison and from judgment: and who shall declare his generation? for he was cut off out of the land of the living: for the transgression of my people

was he stricken.9 And he made his grave with the wicked, and with the rich in his death; because he had done no violence, neither was any deceit in his mouth.10 Yet it pleased the Lord to bruise him; he hath put him to grief: when thou shalt make his soul an offering for sin, he shall see his seed, he shall prolong his days, and the pleasure of the Lord shall prosper in his hand.11 He shall see of the travail of his soul, and shall be satisfied: by his knowledge shall my righteous servant justify many; for he shall bear their iniquities.12 Therefore will I divide him a portion with the great, and he shall divide the spoil with the strong; because he hath poured out his soul unto death: and he was numbered with the transgressors; and he bare the sin of many, and made intercession for the transgressors.

*Prov 4:20-22 My son, attend to my words; incline thine ear unto my sayings....Let them not depart from thine eyes; keep them in the midst of thine heart....For they are life unto those that find them, and health to all their flesh.

*3 John 1:2 Beloved, I wish above all things that thou mayest prosper and be in health, even as thy soul prospereth.

*1 John 5:14-15 And this is the confidence that we have in him, that, if we ask any thing according to his will, he heareth us:...And if we know that he hear us, whatsoever we ask, we know that we have the petitions that we desired of him.

*Mal 3:6 For I am the LORD, I change not; therefore ye sons of Jacob are not consumed.

*Isa 41:10 Fear thou not; for I am with thee: be not dismayed; for I am thy God: I will strengthen thee; yea, I will help thee; yea, I will uphold thee with the right hand of my righteousness.

*Deut 7:15 And the LORD will take away from thee all sickness, and will put none of the evil diseases of Egypt, which thou knowest, upon thee; but will lay them upon all them that hate thee.

*Exo 15:26 And said, If thou wilt diligently hearken to the voice of the LORD thy God, and wilt do that which is right in his sight, and wilt give ear to his commandments, and keep all his statutes, I will put none of these diseases upon thee, which I have brought upon the Egyptians: for I am the LORD that healeth thee.

*Jer 30:17 For I will restore health unto thee, and I will heal thee of thy wounds, saith the LORD;

*Jer 33:6 Behold, I will bring it health and cure, and I will cure them, and will reveal unto them the abundance of peace and truth.

*Deut 30:19-20 I call heaven and earth to record this day against you, that I have set before you life and death, blessing and cursing: therefore choose life, that both thou and thy seed may live:…That thou mayest love the LORD thy God, and that thou mayest obey his voice, and that thou mayest cleave unto him: for he is thy life, and the length of thy days: that thou mayest dwell in the land which the LORD sware unto thy fathers, to Abraham, to Isaac, and to Jacob, to give them.

*Isa 58:8 Then shall thy light break forth as the morning, and thine health shall spring forth speedily: and thy righteousness shall go before thee; the glory of the LORD shall be thy rereward.

*2 Chr 30:20 And the LORD hearkened to Hezekiah, and healed the people.

*Num 23:19 God is not a man, that he should lie; neither the son of man, that he should repent: hath he said, and shall he not do it? or hath he spoken, and shall he not make it good?

*Psa 105:37 He brought them forth also with silver and gold: and there was not one feeble person among their tribes.

*Psa 103:3 Who forgiveth all thine iniquities; who healeth all thy diseases;

*Psa 147:3 He healeth the broken in heart, and bindeth up their wounds.

*Psa 30:2 O LORD my God, I cried unto thee, and thou hast healed me.

*Psa 34:19 Many are the afflictions of the righteous: but the LORD delivereth him out of them all.

*Psa 42:11 Why art thou cast down, O my soul? and why art thou disquieted within me? hope thou in God: for I shall yet praise him, who is the health of my countenance, and my God.

*Mat 8:17 That it might be fulfilled which was spoken by Esaias the prophet, saying, Himself took our infirmities, and bare our sicknesses.

*1 Pet 2:24 Who his own self bare our sins in his own body on the tree, that we, being dead to sins, should live unto righteousness: by whose stripes ye were healed.

*Gal 3:13,14, Christ hath redeemed us from the curse of the law, being made a curse for us: for it is written, Cursed is every one that hangeth on a tree:...

*Prov 3:1-2 My son, forget not my law; but let thine heart keep my commandments:....For length of days, and long life, and peace, shall they add to thee.

*Mat 4:23-24 And Jesus went about all Galilee, teaching in their synagogues, and preaching the gospel of the kingdom, and healing all manner of sickness and all manner of disease among the people....And his fame went throughout all Syria: and they brought unto him all sick people that were taken with divers diseases and torments, and those which were possessed with devils, and those which were lunatic, and those that had the palsy; and he healed them.

*Mat 12:15 But when Jesus knew it, he withdrew himself from thence: and great multitudes followed him, and he healed them all;

*John 10:10 The thief cometh not, but for to steal, and to kill, and to destroy: I am come that they might have life, and that they might have it more abundantly.

*Acts 10:38 How God anointed Jesus of Nazareth with the Holy Ghost and with power: who went about doing good, and healing all that were oppressed of the devil; for God was with him.

*1 John 3:8 He that committeth sin is of the devil; for the devil sinneth from the beginning. For this purpose the Son of God was manifested, that he might destroy the works of the devil.

*Mat 10:1 And when he had called unto him his twelve disciples, he gave them power against unclean spirits, to cast them out, and to heal all manner of sickness and all manner of disease.

*John 14:12-15 Verily, verily, I say unto you, He that believeth on me, the works that I do shall he do also; and greater works than these shall he do; because I go unto my Father….And whatsoever ye shall ask in my name, that will I do, that the Father may be glorified in the Son….If ye shall ask any thing in my name, I will do it….If ye love me, keep my commandments.

*James 5:14-16 Is any sick among you? let him call for the elders of the church; and let them pray over him, anointing him with oil in the name of the Lord:…And the prayer of faith shall save the sick, and the Lord shall raise him up; and if he have committed sins, they shall be forgiven him….Confess your faults one to another, and pray one for another, that ye may be healed. The effectual fervent prayer of a righteous man availeth much.

*Mal 4:2 But unto you that fear my name shall the Sun of righteousness arise with healing in his wings; and ye shall go forth, and grow up as calves of the stall.

*Psa 107:20 He sent his word, and healed them, and delivered them from their destructions.

*Isa 55:11 So shall my word be that goeth forth out of my mouth: it shall not return unto me void, but it shall accomplish that which I please, and it shall prosper in the thing whereto I sent it.

*Luke 4: 18 The Spirit of the Lord is upon me, because he hath anointed me to preach the gospel to the poor; he hath sent me to heal the brokenhearted, to preach deliverance to the captives, and recovering of sight to the blind, to set at liberty them that are bruised, 19 to preach the acceptable year of the Lord.

PRAYER

*Philippians 4:6 - Be careful for nothing; but in every thing by prayer and supplication with thanksgiving let your requests be made known unto God.

*1 Thessalonians 5:17 - Pray without ceasing.

*Mark 11:24 - Therefore I say unto you, What things soever ye desire, when ye pray, believe that ye receive [them], and ye shall have [them].

*Ephesians 6:18 - Praying always with all prayer and supplication in the Spirit, and watching thereunto with all perseverance and supplication for all saints;

*James 5:16 - Confess [your] faults one to another, and pray one for another, that ye may be healed. The effectual fervent prayer of a righteous man availeth much.

*Romans 8:26 - Likewise the Spirit also helpeth our infirmities: for we know not what we should pray for as we ought: but the Spirit itself maketh intercession for us with groanings which cannot be uttered.

*Matthew 21:22 - And all things, whatsoever ye shall ask in prayer, believing, ye shall receive.

*1 John 5:14-15 - And this is the confidence that we have in him, that, if we ask any thing according to his will, he heareth us:

*Colossians 4:2 - Continue in prayer, and watch in the same with thanksgiving;

---

*Psalms 55:17 - Evening, and morning, and at noon, will I pray, and cry aloud: and he shall hear my voice.

---

*Matthew 18:19 - Again I say unto you, That if two of you shall agree on earth as touching anything that they shall ask, it shall be done for them of my Father which is in heaven.

---

*Hebrews 4:16 - Let us therefore come boldly unto the throne of grace, that we may obtain mercy, and find grace to help in time of need.

---

*Matthew 26:39 - And he went a little further, and fell on his face, and prayed, saying, O my Father, if it be possible, let this cup pass from me: nevertheless not as I will, but as thou [wilt].

---

*Isaiah 55:6 - Seek ye the LORD while he may be found, call ye upon him while he is near:

---

*2 Chronicles 7:14 - If my people, which are called by my name, shall humble themselves, and pray, and seek my face, and turn from their wicked ways; then will I hear from heaven, and will forgive their sin, and will heal their land.

---

*Matthew 7:7 - Ask, and it shall be given you; seek, and ye shall find; knock, and it shall be opened unto you:

---

*Psalms 55:16 - As for me, I will call upon God; and the LORD shall save me.

---

*1 Timothy 2:8 - I will therefore that men pray every where, lifting up holy hands, without wrath and doubting.

*1 Thessalonians 5:18 - In every thing give thanks: for this is the will of God in Christ Jesus concerning you.

*James 4:8 - Draw nigh to God, and he will draw nigh to you. Cleanse [your] hands, [ye] sinners; and purify [your] hearts, [ye] double minded.

*John 16:24 - Hitherto have ye asked nothing in my name: ask, and ye shall receive, that your joy may be full.

*James 5:17 - Elias was a man subject to like passions as we are, and he prayed earnestly that it might not rain: and it rained not on the earth by the space of three years and six months.

*Romans 8:26-27 - Likewise the Spirit also helpeth our infirmities: for we know not what we should pray for as we ought: but the Spirit itself maketh intercession for us with groanings which cannot be uttered.   (Read More...)

*Hebrews 11:6 - But without faith [it is] impossible to please [him]: for he that cometh to God must believe that he is, and [that] he is a rewarder of them that diligently seek him.

*John 16:23 - And in that day ye shall ask me nothing. Verily, verily, I say unto you, Whatsoever ye shall ask the Father in my name, he will give [it] you.

*Romans 10:13 - For whosoever shall call upon the name of the Lord shall be saved.

*John 15:16 - Ye have not chosen me, but I have chosen you, and ordained you, that ye should go and bring forth fruit, and

[that] your fruit should remain: that whatsoever ye shall ask of the Father in my name, he may give it you.

---

*Jude 1:20 - But ye, beloved, building up yourselves on your most holy faith, praying in the Holy Ghost,

The Deity of Christ

Matthew 4:10 Then saith Jesus unto him, Get thee hence, Satan: for it is written, Thou shalt worship the Lord thy God, and him only shalt thou serve.

Matthew 28:9 And as they went to tell his disciples, behold, Jesus met them, saying, All hail. And they came and held him by the feet, and worshipped him.

Mark 5:6 But when he saw Jesus afar off, he ran and worshipped him,

---

John 1:1 - In the beginning was the Word, and the Word was with God, and the Word was God.2 The same was in the beginning with God.3 All things were made by him; and without him was not any thing made that was made.

John 1:14 - And the Word was made flesh, and dwelt among us, (and we beheld his glory, the glory as of the only begotten of the Father,) full of grace and truth.

John 1:18 - No man hath seen God at any time; the only begotten Son, which is in the bosom of the Father, he hath declared [him].

John 8:58 - Jesus said unto them, Verily, verily, I say unto you,

Before Abraham was, I am.

John 10:30 - I and [my] Father are one.

Isaiah 9:6 - For unto us a child is born, unto us a son is given: and the government shall be upon his shoulder: and his name shall be called Wonderful, Counsellor, The mighty God, The everlasting Father, The Prince of Peace.

John 20:28 - And Thomas answered and said unto him, My Lord and my God.

---

1 Corinthians 8:6 - But to us [there is but] one God, the Father, of whom [are] all things, and we in him; and one Lord Jesus Christ, by whom [are] all things, and we by him.

Colossians 1:15 Who is the image of the invisible God, the firstborn of every creature:16 For by him were all things created, that are in heaven, and that are in earth, visible and invisible, whether they be thrones, or dominions, or principalities, or powers: all things were created by him, and for him:17 And he is before all things, and by him all things consist.18 And he is the head of the body, the church: who is the beginning, the firstborn from the dead; that in all things he might have the preeminence.19 For it pleased the Father that in him should all fulness dwell;

Titus 2:13 Looking for that blessed hope, and the glorious appearing of the great God and our Saviour Jesus Christ;

Hebrews 1:3 Who being the brightness of his glory, and the express image of his person, and upholding all things by the word of his power, when he had by himself purged our sins, sat down on the right hand of the Majesty on high:

Isaiah 40:3 The voice of him that crieth in the wilderness, Prepare ye the way of the Lord, make straight in the desert a highway for our God.

Isaiah 44:6 Thus saith the Lord the King of Israel, and his redeemer the Lord of hosts; I am the first, and I am the last; and beside me there is no God.

Revelation 1:8 I am Alpha and Omega, the beginning and the ending, saith the Lord, which is, and which was, and which is to come, the Almighty.

2 Peter 1:1 Simon Peter, a servant and an apostle of Jesus Christ, to them that have obtained like precious faith with us through the righteousness of God and our Saviour Jesus Christ:

Revelation 15:3 And they sing the song of Moses the servant of God, and the song of the Lamb, saying, Great and marvellous are thy works, Lord God Almighty; just and true are thy ways, thou King of saints.

Psalm 8:1 O Lord, our Lord, how excellent is thy name in all the earth! who hast set thy glory above the heavens.

Psalm 95:3 For the Lord is a great God, and a great King above all gods.

Christ The Prophet

A prophet of God is someone who reveals God, speaks for God, and communicates to people the truths that God wants them to know. Undoubtedly, Jesus did this when he came to do the will of the Father (Luke 22:42), to reveal the Father (Matt. 11:27), and to speak the things of the Father (John 8:28; 12:49).

Deuteronomy 18:15 The Lord thy God will raise up unto thee a Prophet from the midst of thee, of thy brethren, like unto me; unto him ye shall hearken;

Acts 3:22 For Moses truly said unto the fathers, A prophet shall the Lord your God raise up unto you of your brethren, like unto me; him shall ye hear in all things whatsoever he shall say unto you. 23 And it shall come to pass, that every soul, which will not hear that prophet, shall be destroyed from among the people.

Acts 7:37 This is that Moses, which said unto the children of Israel, A prophet shall the Lord your God raise up unto you of your brethren, like unto me; him shall ye hear.

Luke 13:33 Nevertheless I must walk to day, and to morrow, and the day following: for it cannot be that a prophet perish out of Jerusalem.

Matthew 13:57 And they were offended in him. But Jesus said unto them, A prophet is not without honour, save in his own country, and in his own house.

Christ The Priest

The priests were the ones in the Old Testament who offered sacrifices to God in order to cleanse of sin. Ultimately, all such priests were representations of **Jesus** who is the True **Priest** who offered himself as a sacrifice (Eph. 5:2; Heb. 9:26-27; 10:12) by which he cleanses us of our sin (1 John 1:7). **Jesus** is called a priest after the order of Melchizedek. "Where **Jesus** has entered as a forerunner for us, having become a high priest forever according to the order of Melchizedek."

1 Timothy 2:5 For there is one God, and one mediator between God and men, the man Christ Jesus;

Hebrews 3:1 Wherefore, holy brethren, partakers of the heavenly calling, consider the Apostle and High Priest of our profession, Christ Jesus;

Hebrews 4:14 Seeing then that we have a great high priest, that is passed into the heavens, Jesus the Son of God, let us hold fast our profession.

Hebrews 5:6 As he saith also in another place, Thou art a priest for ever after the order of Melchisedec.

Hebrews 5:10 Called of God an high priest after the order of Melchisedec.

Hebrews 6:20 Whither the forerunner is for us entered, even Jesus, made an high priest for ever after the order of Melchisedec.

Hebrews 7:21 (For those priests were made without an oath; but this with an oath by him that said unto him, The Lord sware and will not repent, Thou art a priest for ever after the order of Melchisedec:)

Hebrews 7:25 Wherefore he is able also to save them to the uttermost that come unto God by him, seeing he ever liveth to make intercession for them.26 For such an high priest became us, who is holy, harmless, undefiled, separate from sinners, and made higher than the heavens;27 Who needeth not daily, as those high priests, to offer up sacrifice, first for his own sins, and then for the people's: for this he did once, when he offered up himself.

Hebrews 8:1 Now of the things which we have spoken this is the sum: We have such an high priest, who is set on the right hand of the throne of the Majesty in the heavens;

Hebrews 9:11 But Christ being come an high priest of good things to come, by a greater and more perfect tabernacle, not made with hands, that is to say, not of this building;

Hebrews 9:24 For Christ is not entered into the holy places made with hands, which are the figures of the true; but into heaven itself, now to appear in the presence of God for us:

Christ The King

A king is someone who has authority to rule and reign over a group of people. Jesus is just such a king. He is called the King of the Jews by the Magi (Matt. 2:2), and Jesus accepts that title in Matt. 27:11, "Now Jesus stood before the governor, and the governor questioned Him, saying, 'Are You the King of the Jews?' And Jesus said to him, 'It is as you say.'"

Matthew 2:2 Saying, Where is he that is born King of the Jews? for we have seen his star in the east, and are come to worship him.

Matthew 21:5 Tell ye the daughter of Sion, Behold, thy King cometh unto thee, meek, and sitting upon an ass, and a colt the foal of an ass.

Matthew 27:11 And Jesus stood before the governor: and the governor asked him, saying, Art thou the King of the Jews? And Jesus said unto him, Thou sayest.

Revelation 15:3 And they sing the song of Moses the servant of God, and the song of the Lamb, saying, Great and marvellous are thy works, Lord God Almighty; just and true are thy ways, thou King of saints.

Revelation 17:14 These shall make war with the Lamb, and the Lamb shall overcome them: for he is Lord of lords, and King of kings: and they that are with him are called, and chosen, and faithful.

Revelation 19:11 And I saw heaven opened, and behold a white horse; and he that sat upon him was called Faithful and True, and in righteousness he doth judge and make war.14 And the armies which were in heaven followed him upon white horses, clothed in fine linen, white and clean.

Revelation 19:16 And he hath on his vesture and on his thigh a name written, King Of Kings, And Lord Of Lords.

Psalm 95:3 For the Lord is a great God, and a great King above all gods.

CHAPTER SIX
JESUS OUR SHEPHERD

Being led by the spirit of God is one of the most important aspects of a believer's life. I cannot tell you how many times my life has been spared because I heard the voice of God. Jesus is very emphatic when he declares that my sheep hear my voice, and another they will not follow. It is extremely important that we become very sensitive to what God is saying to us 1st of all through his word. I actually have written a book about the 20 ways in which God leads and guides his people. Of course one of the major ways that God speaks to us is through his word. As you hide the Scriptures in your heart, meditating upon them, they will become alive on the inside of you. The Holy Spirit will use them to lead and guide you in the exact direction that you need to hear from the heavenly father.

Matthew 16:24 Then said Jesus unto his disciples, If any man will come after me, let him deny himself, and take up his cross, and follow me.

Luke 9:23 And he said to them all, If any man will come after me, let him deny himself, and take up his cross daily, and follow me

John 5:25 Verily, verily, I say unto you, The hour is coming, and now is, when the dead shall hear the voice of the Son of God: and they that hear shall live.

John 8:43 Why do ye not understand my speech? even because ye cannot hear my word.

John 10:3 To him the porter openeth; and the sheep hear his voice: and he calleth his own sheep by name, and leadeth them out.4 And when he putteth forth his own sheep, he goeth before them, and the sheep follow him: for they know his voice.

John 10:9 I am the door: by me if any man enter in, he shall be saved, and shall go in and out, and find pasture.

John 10:14 I am the good shepherd, and know my sheep, and am known of mine.

John 10:16 And other sheep I have, which are not of this fold: them also I must bring, and they shall hear my voice; and there shall be one fold, and one shepherd.

John 10:27 My sheep hear my voice, and I know them, and they follow me:

John 12:26 If any man serve me, let him follow me; and where I am, there shall also my servant be: if any man serve me, him will my Father honour.

John 16:13 Howbeit when he, the Spirit of truth, is come, he will guide you into all truth: for he shall not speak of himself; but whatsoever he shall hear, that shall he speak: and he will shew you things to come.14 He shall glorify me: for he shall receive of mine, and shall shew it unto you.

John 21:22 Jesus saith unto him, If I will that he tarry till I come, what is that to thee? follow thou me.

Acts 3:23 And it shall come to pass, that every soul, which will not hear that prophet, shall be destroyed from among the people.

1 Peter 2:25 For ye were as sheep going astray; but are now returned unto the Shepherd and Bishop of your souls.*Psalms 32:8 - I will instruct thee and teach thee in the way which thou shalt go: I will guide thee with mine eye.

*John 16:13 - Howbeit when he, the Spirit of truth, is come, he will guide you into all truth: for he shall not speak of himself; but whatsoever he shall hear, [that] shall he speak: and he will shew you things to come.

Revelation 3:20 Behold, I stand at the door, and knock: if any man hear my voice, and open the door, I will come in to him, and will sup with him, and he with me.

*Proverbs 3:5-6 - Trust in the LORD with all thine heart; and lean not unto thine own understanding. 6 In all thy ways acknowledge him, and he shall direct thy paths.

*Psalms 119:105 Thy word [is] a lamp unto my feet, and a light unto my path.

*Psalm 18:28 For thou wilt light my candle: the Lord my God will enlighten my darkness.

*Amos 3:7 Surely the Lord God will do nothing, but he revealeth his secret unto his servants the prophets.

*John 15:15 Henceforth I call you not servants; for the servant knoweth not what his lord doeth: but I have called you friends; for all things that I have heard of my Father I have made known unto you.

*Psalm 25:14 The secret of the Lord is with them that fear him; and he will shew them his covenant.

*Jeremiah 23:22 But if they had stood in my counsel, and had caused my people to hear my words, then they should have turned them from their evil way, and from the evil of their doings.

*1 Corinthians 14:24 But if all prophesy, and there come in one that believeth not, or one unlearned, he is convinced of all, he is judged of all: 25 and thus are the secrets of his heart made manifest; and so falling down on his face he will worship God, and report that God is in you of a truth.

*John 14:26 - But the Comforter, [which is] the Holy Ghost, whom the Father will send in my name, he shall teach you all things, and bring all things to your remembrance, whatsoever I have said unto you.

*James 1:5-6 - If any of you lack wisdom, let him ask of God, that giveth to all [men] liberally, and upbraideth not; and it shall be given him.

*Psalms 37:23-24 - The steps of a [good] man are ordered by the LORD: and he delighteth in his way.

*Psalms 25:9-10 - The meek will he guide in judgment: and the meek will he teach his way.

*2 Timothy 3:16 - All scripture [is] given by inspiration of God, and [is] profitable for doctrine, for reproof, for correction, for instruction in righteousness:

*Isaiah 30:21 - And thine ears shall hear a word behind thee, saying, This [is] the way, walk ye in it, when ye turn to the right hand, and when ye turn to the left.

*Psalms 25:4-5 - Shew me thy ways, O LORD; teach me thy paths.

*1 Peter 4:11 - If any man speak, [let him speak] as the oracles of God; if any man minister, [let him do it] as of the ability which God giveth: that God in all things may be glorified through Jesus Christ, to whom be praise and dominion for ever and ever. Amen.

*Psalms 37:23 - The steps of a [good] man are ordered by the LORD: and he delighteth in his way.

*Psalms 25:5-9 - Lead me in thy truth, and teach me: for thou [art] the God of my salvation; on thee do I wait all the day.

*1 Corinthians 1:30 - But of him are ye in Christ Jesus, who of God is made unto us wisdom, and righteousness, and sanctification, and redemption:

*Psalms 25:12-15 - What man [is] he that feareth the LORD? him shall he teach in the way [that] he shall choose.

*Job 33:14-15 - For God speaketh once, yea twice, [yet man] perceiveth it not.

*Isaiah 11:2 - And the spirit of the LORD shall rest upon him, the spirit of wisdom and understanding, the spirit of counsel and might, the spirit of knowledge and of the fear of the LORD;

*Psalm 73:24 Thou shalt guide me with thy counsel, and afterward receive me to glory.

*Isaiah 58:11 and the Lord shall guide thee continually, and satisfy thy soul in drought, and make fat thy bones: and thou shalt be like a watered garden, and like a spring of water, whose waters fail not.

*Luke 1:78 through the tender mercy of our God; whereby the dayspring from on high hath visited us,79 to give light to them that sit in darkness and in the shadow of death, to guide our feet into the way of peace.

   *Proverbs 6:21 bind them continually upon thine heart, and tie them about thy neck.22 When thou goest, it shall lead thee; when thou sleepest, it shall keep thee; and when thou awakest, it shall talk with thee.23 For the commandment is a lamp; and the law is light; and reproofs of instruction are the way of life:

   *Isaiah 42:16 And I will bring the blind by a way that they knew not; I will lead them in paths that they have not known: I will make darkness light before them, and crooked things straight. These things will I do unto them, and not forsake them.

   *Matthew 6:13 And lead us not into temptation, but deliver us from evil: For thine is the kingdom, and the power, and the glory, for ever. Amen.

   *Revelation 7: 16 They shall hunger no more, neither thirst any more; neither shall the sun light on them, nor any heat.17 For the Lamb which is in the midst of the throne shall feed them, and shall lead them unto living fountains of waters: and God shall wipe away all tears from their eyes.

   *Proverbs 3:5 Trust in the Lord with all thine heart; and lean not unto thine own understanding.6 In all thy ways acknowledge him, and he shall direct thy paths.

   *Jeremiah 10:23 O Lord, I know that the way of man is not in himself: it is not in man that walketh to direct his steps.

*2 Peter 1:21 For the prophecy came not in old time by the will of man: but holy men of God spake as they were moved by the Holy Ghost.

*Romans 8:14 For as many as are led by the Spirit of God, they are the sons of God.

*Romans 8:5 For they that are after the flesh do mind the things of the flesh; but they that are after the Spirit the things of the Spirit.

*Psalm 143:10 Teach me to do thy will; for thou art my God: thy spirit is good; lead me into the land of uprightness.

*Proverbs 8:20 I lead in the way of righteousness, in the midst of the paths of judgment:

*Proverbs 20:27 The spirit of man is the candle of the Lord, searching all the inward parts of the belly.

*Psalm 16:11 Thou wilt shew me the path of life: in thy presence is fulness of joy; at thy right hand there are pleasures for evermore.

CHRIST SUFFERINGS

Matthew 20:28 Even as the Son of man came not to be ministered unto, but to minister, and to give his life a ransom for many.

Acts 5:31Him hath God exalted with his right hand to be a Prince and a Saviour, for to give repentance to Israel, and forgiveness of sins.

John 10:18No man taketh it from me, but I lay it down of myself. I have power to lay it down, and I have power to take it again. This commandment have I received of my Father.

Romans 8:37 Nay, in all these things we are more than conquerors through him that loved us.

2 Corinthians 8:9 For ye know the grace of our Lord Jesus Christ, that, though he was rich, yet for your sakes he became poor, that ye through his poverty might be rich.

Galatians 4:4 But when the fulness of the time was come, God sent forth his Son, made of a woman, made under the law,5 To redeem them that were under the law, that we might receive the adoption of sons.6 And because ye are sons, God hath sent forth the Spirit of his Son into your hearts, crying, Abba, Father.7 Wherefore thou art no more a servant, but a son; and if a son, then an heir of God through Christ.

Ephesians 2:4 But God, who is rich in mercy, for his great love wherewith he loved us,

Ephesians 5:2 And walk in love, as Christ also hath loved us, and hath given himself for us an offering and a sacrifice to God for a sweetsmelling savour.

2 Thessalonians 2:16 Now our Lord Jesus Christ himself, and God, even our Father, which hath loved us, and hath given us everlasting consolation and good hope through grace,

1 Timothy 2:6 Who gave himself a ransom for all, to be testified in due time.

Titus 2:14 Who gave himself for us, that he might redeem us from all iniquity, and purify unto himself a peculiar people, zealous of good works.

Hebrews 2:10 For it became him, for whom are all things, and by whom are all things, in bringing many sons unto glory, to make the captain of their salvation perfect through sufferings.

Hebrews 2:14Forasmuch then as the children are partakers of flesh and blood, he also himself likewise took part of the same; that through death he might destroy him that had the power of death, that is, the devil;

Hebrews 9:14 How much more shall the blood of Christ, who through the eternal Spirit offered himself without spot to God, purge your conscience from dead works to serve the living God?

Hebrews 9:26 For then must he often have suffered since the foundation of the world: but now once in the end of the world hath he appeared to put away sin by the sacrifice of himself.27 And as it is appointed unto men once to die, but after this the judgment:

Hebrews 10:10 By the which will we are sanctified through the offering of the body of Jesus Christ once for all.11 And every priest standeth daily ministering and offering oftentimes the same sacrifices, which can never take away sins:12 But this man, after he had offered one sacrifice for sins for ever, sat down on the right hand of God;

Hebrews 12:2 Looking unto Jesus the author and finisher of our faith; who for the joy that was set before him endured the cross, despising the shame, and is set down at the right hand of the throne of God.

1 Peter 2:21 For even hereunto were ye called: because Christ also suffered for us, leaving us an example, that ye should follow his steps:22 Who did no sin, neither was guile found in his mouth:23 Who, when he was reviled, reviled not again; when he suffered, he threatened not; but committed himself to him that judgeth righteously:24 Who his own self bare our sins in his own body on the tree, that we, being dead to sins, should live unto righteousness: by whose stripes ye were healed.

*1 Peter 4:13 - But rejoice, inasmuch as ye are partakers of Christ's sufferings; that, when his glory shall be revealed, ye may be glad also with exceeding joy.

1 John 2:12 I write unto you, little children, because your sins are forgiven you for his name's sake.

1 John 3:16 Hereby perceive we the love of God, because he laid down his life for us: and we ought to lay down our lives for the brethren.

1 John 4:10 Herein is love, not that we loved God, but that he loved us, and sent his Son to be the propitiation for our sins.

Revelation 1:5 And from Jesus Christ, who is the faithful witness, and the first begotten of the dead, and the prince of the kings of the earth. Unto him that loved us, and washed us from our sins in his own blood,

Revelation 5:7 And he came and took the book out of the right hand of him that sat upon the throne.8 And when he had taken the book, the four beasts and four and twenty elders fell down before the Lamb, having every one of them harps, and golden vials full of odours, which are the prayers of saints.9 And they sung a new song, saying, Thou art worthy to take the book, and to open the seals thereof: for thou wast slain, and hast redeemed us to God by thy blood out of every kindred, and tongue, and people, and nation;10 And hast made us unto our God kings and priests: and we shall reign on the earth.11 And I beheld, and I heard the voice of many angels round about the throne and the beasts and the elders: and the number of them was ten thousand times ten thousand, and thousands of thousands;12 Saying with a loud voice, Worthy is the Lamb that was slain to receive power, and riches, and wisdom, and strength, and honour, and glory, and blessing.13 And every creature which is in heaven, and on the earth, and under the earth, and such as are in the sea, and all that are in them, heard I saying, Blessing, and honour, and glory, and power, be unto him that sitteth upon the throne, and unto the Lamb for ever and ever.14 And the four beasts said, Amen. And the four and twenty elders fell down and worshipped him that liveth for ever and ever.

Christ Our Protector

*Psalm 34:19 Many are the afflictions of the righteous: but the Lord delivereth him out of them all.

*Isaiah 54:17 - No weapon that is formed against thee shall prosper; and every tongue [that] shall rise against thee in judgment thou shalt condemn. This [is] the heritage of the servants of the LORD, and their righteousness [is] of me, saith the LORD.

---

*2 Samuel 22:3 the God of my rock; in him will I trust: he is my shield, and the horn of my salvation, my high tower, and my refuge, my saviour; thou savest me from violence.

---

*Psalms 91:1 He that dwelleth in the secret place of the most High shall abide under the shadow of the Almighty.

---

*Psalm 4:8 I will both lay me down in peace, and sleep: for thou, Lord, only makest me dwell in safety.

---

*Jude 1:24-25 - Now unto him that is able to keep you from falling, and to present [you] faultless before the presence of his glory with exceeding joy,

---

*Psalm 62:2 He only is my rock and my salvation; he is my defence; I shall not be greatly moved.

---

*Isaiah 26:3-4 - Thou wilt keep [him] in perfect peace, [whose] mind [is] stayed [on thee]: because he trusteth in thee.

---

*Psalm 91:4 He shall cover thee with his feathers, and under his wings shalt thou trust: his truth shall be thy shield and buckler.

---

*1 Peter 2:9 - But ye [are] a chosen generation, a royal priesthood, an holy nation, a peculiar people; that ye should shew forth the praises of him who hath called you out of darkness into his marvellous light:

---

*John 10:10 - The thief cometh not, but for to steal, and to kill, and to destroy: I am come that they might have life, and that they might have [it] more abundantly.

*John 8:32 - And ye shall know the truth, and the truth shall make you free.

*Psalms 121:1 I will lift up mine eyes unto the hills, from whence cometh my help.

*Psalms 46:1 God [is] our refuge and strength, a very present help in trouble.

*Hebrews 4:16 - Let us therefore come boldly unto the throne of grace, that we may obtain mercy, and find grace to help in time of need.

*1 John 3:8 ..... For this purpose the Son of God was manifested, that he might destroy the works of the devil.

*Philippians 4:19 - But my God shall supply all your need according to his riches in glory by Christ Jesus.

*Ephesians 1:3 - Blessed [be] the God and Father of our Lord Jesus Christ, who hath blessed us with all spiritual blessings in heavenly [places] in Christ:

*Isaiah 43:2 When thou passest through the waters, I will be with thee; and through the rivers, they shall not overflow thee: when thou walkest through the fire, thou shalt not be burned; neither shall the flame kindle upon thee.

PROPHECIES ABOUT CHRIST

Over 350 Prophecies Fulfilled in Jesus Christ

"Lo, I come: in the volume of the book it is written of me" (Psalm 40:7).
"The testimony of Jesus is the spirit of prophecy" (Revelation 19:10).
"...all things must be fulfilled, which were written in the law of Moses, and in the prophets, and in the psalms, concerning me" (Jesus Christ, Luke 24:44).
"And beginning at Moses and all the prophets, he expounded unto them in all the scriptures the things concerning himself." (Jesus Christ, Luke 24:27).
"For had ye believed Moses, ye would have believed me: for he wrote of me." (Jesus Christ, John 5:46). "To Him give all the prophets witness" (Acts 10:43).

http://www.accordingtothescriptures.org/prophecy/353prophecies.html

Genesis 3:15 And I will put enmity between thee and the woman, and between thy seed and her seed; it shall bruise thy head, and thou shalt bruise his heel.

Daniel 9:24 Seventy weeks are determined upon thy people and upon thy holy city, to finish the transgression, and to make an end of sins, and to make reconciliation for iniquity, and to bring in everlasting righteousness, and to seal up the vision and prophecy, and to anoint the most Holy.

*Isaiah 9:5 For every battle of the warrior is with confused noise, and garments rolled in blood; but this shall be with burning and fuel of fire.6 For unto us a child is born, unto us a son is given: and the government shall be upon his shoulder: and his name shall be called Wonderful, Counsellor, The mighty God, The everlasting Father, The Prince of Peace.7 Of the increase of his government and peace there shall be no end, upon the throne of David, and upon his kingdom, to order it, and to establish it with judgment and with justice from henceforth even for ever. The zeal of the Lord of hosts will perform this.

Psalm 89:12 The north and the south thou hast created them: Tabor and Hermon shall rejoice in thy name.13 Thou hast a mighty arm: strong is thy hand, and high is thy right hand.14 Justice and judgment are the habitation of thy throne: mercy and

truth shall go before thy face...........26 He shall cry unto me, Thou art my father, my God, and the rock of my salvation.27 Also I will make him my firstborn, higher than the kings of the earth.28 My mercy will I keep for him for evermore, and my covenant shall stand fast with him. *(whole Chapter)*

Psalm 2:1Why do the heathen rage, and the people imagine a vain thing?2 The kings of the earth set themselves, and the rulers take counsel together, against the Lord, and against his anointed, saying,3 Let us break their bands asunder, and cast away their cords from us.4 He that sitteth in the heavens shall laugh: the Lord shall have them in derision.5 Then shall he speak unto them in his wrath, and vex them in his sore displeasure.6 Yet have I set my king upon my holy hill of Zion.7 I will declare the decree: the Lord hath said unto me, Thou art my Son; this day have I begotten thee.8 Ask of me, and I shall give thee the heathen for thine inheritance, and the uttermost parts of the earth for thy possession.9 Thou shalt break them with a rod of iron; thou shalt dash them in pieces like a potter's vessel.10 Be wise now therefore, O ye kings: be instructed, ye judges of the earth.11 Serve the Lord with fear, and rejoice with trembling.12 Kiss the Son, lest he be angry, and ye perish from the way, when his wrath is kindled but a little. Blessed are all they that put their trust in him.

---

*Mal 3:6 For I am the LORD, I change not; therefore ye sons of Jacob are not consumed.

Zechariah 12:10 And I will pour upon the house of David, and upon the inhabitants of Jerusalem, the spirit of grace and of supplications: and they shall look upon me whom they have pierced, and they shall mourn for him, as one mourneth for his only son, and shall be in bitterness for him, as one that is in bitterness for his firstborn.

Psalm 22:1 My God, my God, why hast thou forsaken me? why art thou so far from helping me, and from the words of my roaring?.........7 All they that see me laugh me to scorn: they shoot out the lip, they shake the head, saying,8 He trusted on the Lord that he would deliver him: let him deliver him, seeing he delighted in him..........12 Many bulls have compassed me: strong bulls of Bashan have beset me round.13 They gaped upon me with their mouths, as a ravening and a roaring lion.14 I am poured out like water, and all my bones are out of joint: my heart is like wax; it is melted in the midst of my bowels.15 My strength is dried up like a potsherd; and my tongue cleaveth to my jaws; and thou hast brought me into the dust of death.16 For dogs have compassed me: the assembly of the wicked have inclosed me: they pierced my hands and my feet.17 I may tell all my bones: they look and stare upon me.18 They part my garments among them, and cast lots upon my vesture.19 But be not thou far from me, O Lord: O my strength, haste thee to help me.........22 I will declare thy name unto my brethren: in the midst of the congregation will I praise thee.23 Ye that fear the Lord, praise him; all ye the seed of Jacob, glorify him; and fear him, all ye the seed of Israel.......30 A seed shall serve him; it shall be accounted to the Lord for a generation.31 They shall come, and shall declare his righteousness unto a people that shall be born, that he hath done this.

Zechariah 13:7 Awake, O sword, against my shepherd, and against the man that is my fellow, saith the Lord of hosts: smite the shepherd, and the sheep shall be scattered: and I will turn mine hand upon the little ones.

Revelation 1:7 Behold, he cometh with clouds; and every eye shall see him, and they also which pierced him: and all kindreds of the earth shall wail because of him. Even so, Amen.

Revelation 19:10 And I fell at his feet to worship him. And he said unto me, See thou do it not: I am thy fellowservant, and of thy brethren that have the testimony of Jesus: worship God: for the testimony of Jesus is the spirit of prophecy.

CHAPTER SEVEN
AUTHORITY & POWER OF CHRIST

Those who know Christ are called of God to walk in a place of authority and power. These I share with you are powerful Scriptures that we need to meditate upon on a daily basis in order to step into this reality. I have included a combination of old and new Testaments Scriptures that will help you to begin to realize this amazing place where Christ has call us to walk and move.

Matthew 7:28-29And it came to pass, when Jesus had ended these sayings, the people were astonished at his doctrine: For he taught them as one having authority, and not as the scribes.

Matthew 9:6But that ye may know that the Son of man hath power on earth to forgive sins, (then saith he to the sick of the palsy,) Arise, take up thy bed, and go unto thine house.

Matthew 10:1And when he had called unto him his twelve disciples, he gave them power against unclean spirits, to cast them out, and to heal all manner of sickness and all manner of disease.

Matthew 11:27 All things are delivered unto me of my Father: and no man knoweth the Son, but the Father; neither knoweth any man the Father, save the Son, and he to whomsoever the Son will reveal him.

Matthew 26:64Jesus saith unto him, Thou hast said: nevertheless I say unto you, Hereafter shall ye see the Son of man sitting on the right hand of power, and coming in the clouds of heaven.

Matthew 28:18-20 And Jesus came and spake unto them, saying, All power is given unto me in heaven and in earth. Go ye therefore, and teach all nations, baptizing them in the name of the Father, and of the Son, and of the Holy Ghost: Teaching them to observe all things whatsoever I have commanded you: and, lo, I am with you alway, even unto the end of the world. Amen.

John 3:31He that cometh from above is above all: he that is of the earth is earthly, and speaketh of the earth: he that cometh from heaven is above all.

John 3:35The Father loveth the Son, and hath given all things into his hand.

John 5:21For as the Father raiseth up the dead, and quickeneth them; even so the Son quickeneth whom he will.

John 17:2As thou hast given him power over all flesh, that he should give eternal life to as many as thou hast given him.

John 5:28-29Marvel not at this: for the hour is coming, in the which all that are in the graves shall hear his voice, And shall come forth; they that have done good, unto the resurrection of life; and they that have done evil, unto the resurrection of damnation.

John 8:23 And he said unto them, Ye are from beneath; I am from above: ye are of this world; I am not of this world.

John 16:33These things I have spoken unto you, that in me ye might have peace. In the world ye shall have tribulation: but be of good cheer; I have overcome the world.

John 17:2As thou hast given him power over all flesh, that he should give eternal life to as many as thou hast given him.

*Acts 1:8 But ye shall receive power, after that the Holy Ghost is come upon you: and ye shall be witnesses unto me both in Jerusalem, and in all Judæa, and in Samaria, and unto the uttermost part of the earth.

Ephesians 1:12 That we should be to the praise of his glory, who first trusted in Christ.13 In whom ye also trusted, after that ye heard the word of truth, the gospel of your salvation: in whom also after that ye believed, ye were sealed with that holy Spirit of promise,14 Which is the earnest of our inheritance until the redemption of the purchased possession, unto the praise of his glory.15 Wherefore I also, after I heard of your faith in the Lord Jesus, and love unto all the saints,16 Cease not to give thanks for you, making mention of you in my prayers;17 That the God of our Lord Jesus Christ, the Father of glory, may give unto you the spirit of wisdom and revelation in the knowledge of him:18 The eyes of your understanding being enlightened; that ye may know what is the hope of his calling, and what the riches of the glory of his inheritance in the saints,19 And what is the exceeding greatness of his power to us-ward who believe, according to the working of his mighty power,And what is the exceeding greatness of his power to us-ward who believe, according to the working of his mighty power, Which he wrought in Christ, when he raised him from the dead, and set him at his own right hand in the heavenly places, Far above all principality, and power, and might, and dominion, and every name that is named, not only in this world, but also in that which is to come:

*Ephesians 3:14 For this cause I bow my knees unto the Father of our Lord Jesus Christ,15 of whom the whole family in heaven and earth is named, 16 that he would grant you, according to the riches of his glory, to be strengthened with might by his Spirit in the inner man; 17 that Christ may dwell in your hearts by faith; that ye, being rooted and grounded in love, 18 may be able to comprehend with all saints what is the breadth, and length, and depth, and height; 19 and to know the love of Christ, which passeth knowledge, that ye might be filled with all the fulness of God.20 Now unto him that is able to do exceeding abundantly above all that we ask or think, according to the power that worketh in us, 21 unto him be glory in the church by Christ Jesus throughout all ages, world without end. Amen.

*Ephesians 4: 8 Wherefore he saith, When he ascended up on high, he led captivity captive, and gave gifts unto men. 9 (Now that he ascended, what is it but that he also descended first into the lower parts of the earth?10 He that descended is the same also that ascended up far above all heavens, that he might fill all things.)

Philippians 2:9Wherefore God also hath highly exalted him, and given him a name which is above every name:10 That at the name of Jesus every knee should bow, of things in heaven, and things in earth, and things under the earth;

*Colossians 1:12 Giving thanks unto the Father, which hath made us meet to be partakers of the inheritance of the saints in light:13 Who hath delivered us from the power of darkness, and hath translated us into the kingdom of his dear Son:14 In whom we have redemption through his blood, even the forgiveness of sins:15 Who is the image of the invisible God, the firstborn of every creature:16 For by him were all things created, that are in heaven, and that are in earth, visible and invisible, whether they be thrones, or dominions, or principalities, or powers: all things were created by him, and for him:17 And he is before all things, and by him all things consist.18 And he is the head of the body, the church: who is the beginning, the firstborn from the dead; that in all things he might have the preeminence.19 For it pleased the Father that in him should all fulness dwell;20 And, having made peace through the blood of his cross, by him to reconcile all things unto himself; by him, I say, whether they be things in earth, or things in heaven.21 And you, that were sometime alienated and enemies in your mind by wicked works, yet now hath he reconciled 22 In the body of his flesh through death, to present you holy and unblameable and unreproveable in his sight:23 If ye continue in the faith grounded and settled, and be not moved away from the hope of the gospel, which ye have heard, and which was preached to every creature which is under heaven; whereof I Paul am made a minister;

---

   *Colossians 2:2 That their hearts might be comforted, being knit together in love, and unto all riches of the full assurance of understanding, to the acknowledgement of the mystery of God, and of the Father, and of Christ;3 In whom are hid all the treasures of wisdom and knowledge.9 For in him (Christ) dwelleth all the fulness of the Godhead bodily. 10 And ye are complete in him, which is the head of all principality and power:..............6 As ye have therefore received Christ Jesus the Lord, so walk ye in him:7 Rooted and built up in him, and stablished in the faith, as ye have been taught, abounding therein with thanksgiving.8 Beware lest any man spoil you through philosophy and vain deceit, after the tradition of men, after the rudiments of the world, and not after Christ.9 For in him dwelleth all the fulness of the Godhead bodily.10 And ye are complete in him, which is the head of all principality and power:11 In whom also ye are circumcised with the circumcision made without hands, in putting off the body of the sins of the flesh by the circumcision of Christ:12 Buried with him in baptism, wherein also ye are risen with him through the faith of the operation of God, who hath raised him from the dead.13 And you, being dead in your sins and the uncircumcision of your flesh, hath he quickened together with him, having forgiven you all trespasses;14 Blotting out the handwriting of ordinances that was against us, which was contrary to us, and took it out of the way, nailing it to his cross;15 And having spoiled principalities and powers, he made a shew of them openly, triumphing over them in it.16 Let no man therefore judge you in meat, or in drink, or in respect of an holyday, or of the new moon, or of the sabbath days:17 Which are a shadow of things to come; but the body is of Christ.

*Hebrews 2:8 thou hast put all things in subjection under his feet. For in that he put all in subjection under him, he left nothing that is not put under him. But now we see not yet all things put under him. 9 But we see Jesus, who was made a little lower than the angels for the suffering of death, crowned with glory and honour; that he by the grace of God should taste death for every man.10 For it became him, for whom are all things, and by whom are all things, in bringing many sons unto glory, to make the captain of their salvation perfect through sufferings.

1 Peter 3: ..... by the resurrection of Jesus Christ:22Who is gone into heaven, and is on the right hand of God; angels and authorities and powers being made subject unto him.

Jude 25 To the only wise God our Saviour, be glory and majesty, dominion and power, both now and ever. Amen.

Psalm 8:6Thou madest him to have dominion over the works of thy hands; thou hast put all things under his feet:

Daniel 7:13I saw in the night visions, and, behold, one like the Son of man came with the clouds of heaven, and came to the Ancient of days, and they brought him near before him.

*Daniel 11:32 ..... but the people that do know their God shall be strong, and do exploits.

*Jeremiah 33:3 call unto me, and I will answer thee, and shew thee great and mighty things, which thou knowest not.

*Isaiah 65:24 And it shall come to pass, that before they call, I will answer; and while they are yet speaking, I will hear.

*Isaiah 55:6 Seek ye the Lord while he may be found, call ye upon him while he is near:7 Let the wicked forsake his way, and the unrighteous man his thoughts: and let him return unto the Lord, and he will have mercy upon him; and to our God, for he will abundantly pardon.

*Isaiah 45:3 And I will give thee the treasures of darkness, and hidden riches of secret places, that thou mayest know that I, the Lord, which call thee by thy name, am the God of Israel.

*Psalm 25:14 The secret of the Lord is with them that fear him; and he will shew them his covenant.

*1 Peter 4:11 If any man speak, let him speak as the oracles of God; if any man minister, let him do it as of the ability which God giveth: that God in all things may be glorified through Jesus Christ, to whom be praise and dominion for ever and ever. Amen.

*Proverbs 28:1 The wicked flee when no man pursueth: but the righteous are bold as a lion.

*2 Samuel 23:2 The Spirit of the Lord spake by me, and his word was in my tongue.

*Acts 10:38 how God anointed Jesus of Nazareth with the Holy Ghost and with power: who went about doing good, and healing all that were oppressed of the devil; for God was with him.

*Matthew 10:8 Heal the sick, cleanse the lepers, raise the dead, cast out devils: freely ye have received, freely give.

*Luke 4:18 The Spirit of the Lord is upon me, because he hath anointed me to preach the gospel to the poor; he hath sent me to heal the brokenhearted, to preach deliverance to the captives, and recovering of sight to the blind, to set at liberty them that are bruised, 19 to preach the acceptable year of the Lord.

---

*Numbers 23:19 God is not a man, that he should lie; neither the son of man, that he should repent: hath he said, and shall he not do it? or hath he spoken, and shall he not make it good?

---

*Acts 6:8 And Stephen, full of faith and power, did great wonders and miracles among the people.

---

*Acts 2:17 And it shall come to pass in the last days, saith God, I will pour out of my Spirit upon all flesh: and your sons and your daughters shall prophesy, and your young men shall see visions, and your old men shall dream dreams:18 And on my servants and on my handmaidens I will pour out in those days of my Spirit; and they shall prophesy:

---

*Luke 10:19 Behold, I give unto you power to tread on serpents and scorpions, and over all the power of the enemy: and nothing shall by any means hurt you.

---

*2 Samuel 22:35 He teacheth my hands to war; so that a bow of steel is broken by mine arms.

---

*Psalm 18:33 He maketh my feet like hinds' feet, and setteth me upon my high places.34 He teacheth my hands to war, so that a bow of steel is broken by mine arms.

---

*Matthew 8:9 For I am a man under authority, having soldiers under me: and I say to this man, Go, and he goeth; and to another, Come, and he cometh; and to my servant, Do this, and he doeth it.

*Mark 1:27 And they were all amazed, insomuch that they questioned among themselves, saying, What thing is this? what new doctrine is this? for with authority commandeth he even the unclean spirits, and they do obey him.

*Luke 9:1 Then he called his twelve disciples together, and gave them power and authority over all devils, and to cure diseases.

Victory In Christ

John 16:33 - These things I have spoken unto you, that in me ye might have peace. In the world ye shall have tribulation: but be of good cheer; I have overcome the world.

James 1:12-14 - Blessed [is] the man that endureth temptation: for when he is tried, he shall receive the crown of life, which the Lord hath promised to them that love him.

Psalms 108:13 - Through God we shall do valiantly: for he [it is that] shall tread down our enemies.

1 Corinthians 10:13 - There hath no temptation taken you but such as is common to man: but God [is] faithful, who will not suffer you to be tempted above that ye are able; but will with the temptation also make a way to escape, that ye may be able to bear [it].

1 Corinthians 15:3 For I delivered unto you first of all that which I also received, how that Christ died for our sins according to the scriptures;4 And that he was buried, and that he rose again the third day according to the scripture.

1 Corinthians 15:57 - But thanks [be] to God, which giveth us the victory through our Lord Jesus Christ.

Romans 8:37 - Nay, in all these things we are more than conquerors through him that loved us.

2 Corinthians 2:14 - Now thanks [be] unto God, which always causeth us to triumph in Christ, and maketh manifest the savour of his knowledge by us in every place.

Philippians 4:13 - I can do all things through Christ which strengtheneth me.

Romans 6:14 - For sin shall not have dominion over you: for ye are not under the law, but under grace.

Romans 8:1-39 - [There is] therefore now no condemnation to them which are in Christ Jesus, who walk not after the flesh, but after the Spirit.

Romans 8:31 - What shall we then say to these things? If God [be] for us, who [can be] against us?

Romans 8:39 - Nor height, nor depth, nor any other creature, shall be able to separate us from the love of God, which is in Christ Jesus our Lord.

Deuteronomy 20:1-4 - When thou goest out to battle against thine enemies, and seest horses, and chariots, [and] a people more than thou, be not afraid of them: for the LORD thy God [is] with thee, which brought thee up out of the land of Egypt.   (Read More...)

Ephesians 6:13 - Wherefore take unto you the whole armour of

God, that ye may be able to withstand in the evil day, and having done all, to stand.

Revelation 21:6-7 - And he said unto me, It is done. I am Alpha and Omega, the beginning and the end. I will give unto him that is athirst of the fountain of the water of life freely.

Ephesians 6:10 - Finally, my brethren, be strong in the Lord, and in the power of his might.

Proverbs 24:16 - For a just [man] falleth seven times, and riseth up again: but the wicked shall fall into mischief.

Revelation 12:10 - And I heard a loud voice saying in heaven, Now is come salvation, and strength, and the kingdom of our God, and the power of his Christ: for the accuser of our brethren is cast down, which accused them before our God day and night.

Colossians 2:15And having spoiled principalities and powers, he made a shew of them openly, triumphing over them in it.

1 John 3:8He that committeth sin is of the devil; for the devil sinneth from the beginning. For this purpose the Son of God was manifested, that he might destroy the works of the devil.

IN CHRIST

John 15:15 - Henceforth I call you not servants; for the servant knoweth not what his lord doeth: but I have called you friends; for all things that I have heard of my Father I have made known unto you.

2 Corinthians 5:17 - Therefore if any man [be] in Christ, [he is] a new creature: old things are passed away; behold, all things are become new.

1 Peter 2:9 - But ye [are] a chosen generation, a royal priesthood, an holy nation, a peculiar people; that ye should shew forth the praises of him who hath called you out of darkness into his marvellous light:

Ephesians 2:10 - For we are his workmanship, created in Christ Jesus unto good works, which God hath before ordained that we should walk in them.

Romans 8:1 - [There is] therefore now no condemnation to them which are in Christ Jesus, who walk not after the flesh, but after the Spirit.

John 1:12 - But as many as received him, to them gave he power to become the sons of God, [even] to them that believe on his name:

2 Corinthians 5:21 - For he hath made him [to be] sin for us, who knew no sin; that we might be made the righteousness of God in him.

1 Corinthians 6:19 - What? know ye not that your body is the

temple of the Holy Ghost [which is] in you, which ye have of God, and ye are not your own?

1 Corinthians 12:27 - Now ye are the body of Christ, and members in particular.

Romans 12:2 - And be not conformed to this world: but be ye transformed by the renewing of your mind, that ye may prove what [is] that good, and acceptable, and perfect, will of God.

1 John 4:4 - Ye are of God, little children, and have overcome them: because greater is he that is in you, than he that is in the world.

*Acts 17:28 For in him we live, and move, and have our being;

*Romans 6:4 Therefore we are buried with him by baptism into death: that like as Christ was raised up from the dead by the glory of the Father, even so we also should walk in newness of life.

*Galatians 6:15 For in Christ Jesus neither circumcision availeth any thing, nor uncircumcision, but a new creature.

Looking Upon Christ

Matthew 5:8 Blessed are the pure in heart: for they shall see God.

Romans 8:29 For whom he did foreknow, he also did predestinate to be conformed to the image of his Son, that he might be the firstborn among many brethren.

1 Corinthians 15:49 And as we have borne the image of the earthy, we shall also bear the image of the heavenly.

2 Corinthians 3:17 Now the Lord is that Spirit: and where the Spirit of the Lord is, there is liberty.18 But we all, with open face beholding as in a glass the glory of the Lord, are changed into the same image from glory to glory, even as by the Spirit of the Lord.

Philippians 3:21 Who shall change our vile body, that it may be fashioned like unto his glorious body, according to the working whereby he is able even to subdue all things unto himself.

Hebrews 12:1 Wherefore seeing we also are compassed about with so great a cloud of witnesses, let us lay aside every weight, and the sin which doth so easily beset us, and let us run with patience the race that is set before us,2 Looking unto Jesus the author and finisher of our faith; who for the joy that was set before him endured the cross, despising the shame, and is set down at the right hand of the throne of God.3 For consider him that endured such contradiction of sinners against himself, lest ye be wearied and faint in your minds.4 Ye have not yet resisted unto blood, striving against sin.

1 John 3:2 Beloved, now are we the sons of God, and it doth not yet appear what we shall be: but we know that, when he shall

appear, we shall be like him; for we shall see him as he is.

Revelation 1:5 And from Jesus Christ, who is the faithful witness, and the first begotten of the dead, and the prince of the kings of the earth. Unto him that loved us, and washed us from our sins in his own blood,6 And hath made us kings and priests unto God and his Father; to him be glory and dominion for ever and ever. Amen.7 Behold, he cometh with clouds; and every eye shall see him, and they also which pierced him: and all kindreds of the earth shall wail because of him. Even so, Amen.8 I am Alpha and Omega, the beginning and the ending, saith the Lord, which is, and which was, and which is to come, the Almighty.

Revelation 1:10 I was in the Spirit on the Lord's day, and heard behind me a great voice, as of a trumpet,11 Saying, I am Alpha and Omega, the first and the last: and, What thou seest, write in a book, and send it unto the seven churches which are in Asia; unto Ephesus, and unto Smyrna, and unto Pergamos, and unto Thyatira, and unto Sardis, and unto Philadelphia, and unto Laodicea.12 And I turned to see the voice that spake with me. And being turned, I saw seven golden candlesticks;13 And in the midst of the seven candlesticks one like unto the Son of man, clothed with a garment down to the foot, and girt about the paps with a golden girdle.14 His head and his hairs were white like wool, as white as snow; and his eyes were as a flame of fire;15 And his feet like unto fine brass, as if they burned in a furnace; and his voice as the sound of many waters.16 And he had in his right hand seven stars: and out of his mouth went a sharp twoedged sword: and his countenance was as the sun shineth in his strength.17 And when I saw him, I fell at his feet as dead. And he laid his right hand upon me, saying unto me, Fear not; I am the first and the last:18 I am he that liveth, and was dead; and, behold, I am alive for evermore, Amen; and have the keys of hell and of death.

Revelation 21:3 And I heard a great voice out of heaven saying, Behold, the tabernacle of God is with men, and he will dwell with them, and they shall be his people, and God himself shall be with them, and be their God.4 And God shall wipe away all tears from their eyes; and there shall be no more death, neither sorrow, nor crying, neither shall there be any more pain: for the former things are passed away.

Revelation 22:4 And they shall see his face; and his name shall be in their foreheads.

Job 19:26 And though after my skin worms destroy this body, yet in my flesh shall I see God:27 Whom I shall see for myself, and mine eyes shall behold, and not another; though my reins be consumed within me.

Psalm 17:15 As for me, I will behold thy face in righteousness: I shall be satisfied, when I awake, with thy likeness.

CHAPTER EIGHT
FAITH, TRUST, BELIEVE,

Faith in **Christ** is the key to our victory! With this truth and reality in our heart, it is expedient that we become full of faith. As we connect the dots from Genesis to Revelation, it becomes quite clear that the cause of all of man's sorrows, shortcomings, immoralities, sicknesses, troubles are due to the fact that we are not truly trusting, looking, depending, relying and having faith in **Christ**! Based upon this fact we must do everything we can to attain more faith. Even the disciples as they watched the life of **Jesus** before their eyes, asked Him to help increase their faith. This is the whole purpose of this book. To provide biblical means by which we can have an increase of faith in **Christ** which causes us to overcome! Please open your heart, your mind, and your life to these realities. And let **Jesus Christ** become your all!

A Brief Description of Faith: It is when God, His Word, His will is Supernaturally Quickened to you by the Holy Spirit! These realities become more real to you than anything in life. **It is a revelation of Who Jesus Christ really is & what He has done and is doing.** It is a quickening in your heart when you know, that you know, that you know, that you know God is with you, then who can be against you? That **Christ Jesus** Himself, lives inside of you. Your mind, your will, your emotions, and every part of your being is overwhelmed with the reality of **Jesus Christ**! And you enter into the realm where all things are possible! This is where, by God's grace that it is my hope and desire to take you.

*Mark 16:16 - He that believeth and is baptized shall be saved; but he that believeth not shall be damned.

John 3:16 - For God so loved the world, that he gave his only begotten Son, that whosoever believeth in him should not perish, but have everlasting life.

*John 3:36 - He that believeth on the Son hath everlasting life: and he that believeth not the Son shall not see life; but the wrath of God abideth on him.

John 6:47 - Verily, verily, I say unto you, He that believeth on me hath everlasting life.

John 5:24 - Verily, verily, I say unto you, He that heareth my word, and believeth on him that sent me, hath everlasting life, and shall not come into condemnation; but is passed from death unto life.

*John 6:35 - And Jesus said unto them, I am the bread of life: he that cometh to me shall never hunger; and he that believeth on me shall never thirst.

John 8:24 - I said therefore unto you, that ye shall die in your sins: for if ye believe not that I am [he], ye shall die in your sins.

*Proverbs 3:Trust in the Lord with all thine heart; and lean not unto thine own understanding. In all thy ways acknowledge him, and he shall direct thy paths.

*2 Corinthians 5:7 - (For we walk by faith, not by sight:)

*Hebrews 11:6 - But without faith [it is] impossible to please [him]: for he that cometh to God must believe that he is, and [that] he is a rewarder of them that diligently seek him.

*1 John 5:4 - For whatsoever is born of God overcometh the world: and this is the victory that overcometh the world, [even] our faith. 5 Who is he that overcometh the world, but he that believeth that Jesus is the Son of God?

*Mark 9:23 - Jesus said unto him, If thou canst believe, all things [are] possible to him that believeth.

*Luke 17:6 - And the Lord said, If ye had faith as a grain of mustard seed, ye might say unto this sycamine tree, Be thou plucked up by the root, and be thou planted in the sea; and it should obey you.

*Hebrews 11:1-39 - Now faith is the substance of things hoped for, the evidence of things not seen.

*1 John 5:14 - And this is the confidence that we have in him, that, if we ask any thing according to his will, he heareth us:

*Psalms 40:4 - Blessed [is] that man that maketh the LORD his trust, and respecteth not the proud, nor such as turn aside to lies.

*Mark 11:23 - For verily I say unto you, That whosoever shall say unto this mountain, Be thou removed, and be thou cast into the sea; and shall not doubt in his heart, but shall believe that those things which he saith shall come to pass; he shall have whatsoever he saith.

Acts 16:31 - And they said, Believe on the Lord Jesus Christ, and thou shalt be saved, and thy house.

*Acts 26:18 - To open their eyes, [and] to turn [them] from darkness to light, and [from] the power of Satan unto God, that they may receive forgiveness of sins, and inheritance among them which are sanctified by faith that is in me.

*James 1:12 - Blessed [is] the man that endureth temptation: for when he is tried, he shall receive the crown of life, which the Lord hath promised to them that love him.

*1 Peter 1:7 - That the trial of your faith, being much more precious than of gold that perisheth, though it be tried with fire, might be found unto praise and honour and glory at the appearing of Jesus Christ:

*Ephesians 6:16 - Above all, taking the shield of faith, wherewith ye shall be able to quench all the fiery darts of the wicked.

Romans 10:9 - That if thou shalt confess with thy mouth the Lord Jesus, and shalt believe in thine heart that God hath raised him from the dead, thou shalt be saved.

*1 Corinthians 2:5 - That your faith should not stand in the wisdom of men, but in the power of God.

*Colossians 2:7 - Rooted and built up in him, and stablished in the faith, as ye have been taught, abounding therein with thanksgiving.

*1 Samuel 17:37 - David said moreover, The LORD that delivered me out of the paw of the lion, and out of the paw of the bear, he will deliver me out of the hand of this Philistine. And Saul said unto David, Go, and the LORD be with thee.

*Revelation 3:20 - Behold, I stand at the door, and knock: if any man hear my voice, and open the door, I will come in to him, and will sup with him, and he with me.

---

*Hebrews 10:39 - But we are not of them who draw back unto perdition; but of them that believe to the saving of the soul.

---

*Romans 8:37 - Nay, in all these things we are more than conquerors through him that loved us.

---

*James 1:6 - But let him ask in faith, nothing wavering. For he that wavereth is like a wave of the sea driven with the wind and tossed.

---

*Hebrews 11:7 - By faith Noah, being warned of God of things not seen as yet, moved with fear, prepared an ark to the saving of his house; by the which he condemned the world, and became heir of the righteousness which is by faith.

---

*2 Timothy 4:7 - I have fought a good fight, I have finished [my] course, I have kept the faith:

---

*Hebrews 12:2 - Looking unto Jesus the author and finisher of [our] faith; who for the joy that was set before him endured the cross, despising the shame, and is set down at the right hand of the throne of God.

---

*1 Timothy 3:9 - Holding the mystery of the faith in a pure conscience.

---

*Colossians 1:23 - If ye continue in the faith grounded and settled, and [be] not moved away from the hope of the gospel, which ye have heard, [and] which was preached to every creature which is under heaven; whereof I Paul am made a minister;

*Romans 10:17 - So then faith [cometh] by hearing, and hearing by the word of God.

*1 Peter 1:8 - Whom having not seen, ye love; in whom, though now ye see [him] not, yet believing, ye rejoice with joy unspeakable and full of glory:

*Colossians 2:7 - Rooted and built up in him, and stablished in the faith, as ye have been taught, abounding therein with thanksgiving.

*Romans 10:9 - That if thou shalt confess with thy mouth the Lord Jesus, and shalt believe in thine heart that God hath raised him from the dead, thou shalt be saved.

*Psalms 60:12 - Through God we shall do valiantly: for he [it is that] shall tread down our enemies.

*Psalms 31:14-15 - But I trusted in thee, O LORD: I said, Thou [art] my God.

*Galatians 5:1 - Stand fast therefore in the liberty wherewith Christ hath made us free, and be not entangled again with the yoke of bondage.

*Isaiah 40:31 - But they that wait upon the LORD shall renew [their] strength; they shall mount up with wings as eagles; they shall run, and not be weary; [and] they shall walk, and not faint.

*Isaiah 26:3-4 - Thou wilt keep [him] in perfect peace, [whose] mind [is] stayed [on thee]: because he trusteth in thee.

*Psalms 37:5-6 - Commit thy way unto the LORD; trust also in him; and he shall bring [it] to pass.

*Psalm 57:1 Be merciful unto me, O God, be merciful unto me: for my soul trusteth in thee: yea, in the shadow of thy wings will I make my refuge, until these calamities be overpast.

*1 Timothy 6:12 Fight the good fight of faith, lay hold on eternal life, whereunto thou art also called, and hast professed a good profession before many witnesses.

Galatians 2:16 - Knowing that a man is not justified by the works of the law, but by the faith of Jesus Christ, even we have believed in Jesus Christ, that we might be justified by the faith of Christ, and not by the works of the law: for by the works of the law shall no flesh be justified.

Ephesians 2:8 - For by grace are ye saved through faith; and that not of yourselves: [it is] the gift of God:

Our Purpose & Calling In CHRIST

*Matthew 4:19 And he saith unto them, Follow me, and I will make you fishers of men.

*Jeremiah 1:5 Before I formed thee in the belly I knew thee; and before thou camest forth out of the womb I sanctified thee, and I ordained thee a prophet unto the nations.

*Philippians 3:14 I press toward the mark for the prize of the high calling of God in Christ Jesus.

*1 Peter 5:2 feed the flock of God which is among you, taking the oversight thereof, not by constraint, but willingly; not for filthy lucre, but of a ready mind;

*2 Timothy 4:2 preach the word; be instant in season, out of season; reprove, rebuke, exhort with all longsuffering and doctrine.

*1 Corinthians 7:20 Let every man abide in the same calling wherein he was called.

*John 15:16 Ye have not chosen me, but I have chosen you, and ordained you, that ye should go and bring forth fruit, and that your fruit should remain: that whatsoever ye shall ask of the Father in my name, he may give it you.

*1 Peter 4:11 If any man speak, let him speak as the oracles of God; if any man minister, let him do it as of the ability which God giveth: that God in all things may be glorified through Jesus Christ, to whom be praise and dominion for ever and ever. Amen.

*Ephesians 1:4 - According as he hath chosen us in him before the foundation of the world, that we should be holy and without blame before him in love: 5 Having predestinated us unto the adoption of children by Jesus Christ to himself, according to the good pleasure of his will,6 To the praise of the glory of his grace, wherein he hath made us accepted in the beloved.7 In whom we have redemption through his blood, the forgiveness of sins, according to the riches of his grace;8 Wherein he hath abounded toward us in all wisdom and prudence;9 Having made known unto us the mystery of his will, according to his good pleasure which he hath purposed in himself:10 That in the dispensation of the fulness of times he might gather together in one all things in Christ, both which are in heaven, and which are on earth; even in

him:11 In whom also we have obtained an inheritance, being predestinated according to the purpose of him who worketh all things after the counsel of his own will:12 That we should be to the praise of his glory, who first trusted in Christ.

*Colossians 2:9 - For in him dwelleth all the fulness of the Godhead bodily.

*Ephesians 4:1-15 - I therefore, the prisoner of the Lord, beseech you that ye walk worthy of the vocation wherewith ye are called,

*1 Corinthians 6:19-20 - What? know ye not that your body is the temple of the Holy Ghost [which is] in you, which ye have of God, and ye are not your own?

*Matthew 6:19-21 - Lay not up for yourselves treasures upon earth, where moth and rust doth corrupt, and where thieves break through and steal:

*Galatians 2:20 - I am crucified with Christ: nevertheless I live; yet not I, but Christ liveth in me: and the life which I now live in the flesh I live by the faith of the Son of God, who loved me, and gave himself for me.

*Luke 16:13 - No servant can serve two masters: for either he will hate the one, and love the other; or else he will hold to the one, and despise the other. Ye cannot serve God and mammon.

*Mark 16:16 - He that believeth and is baptized shall be saved; but he that believeth not shall be damned.

*Genesis 1:27 - So God created man in his [own] image, in the image of God created he him; male and female created he them.

*Romans 12:4 - For as we have many members in one body, and all members have not the same office:

*Jeremiah 29:11 - For I know the thoughts that I think toward you, saith the LORD, thoughts of peace, and not of evil, to give you an expected end.

*1 Peter 2:9 - But ye [are] a chosen generation, a royal priesthood, an holy nation, a peculiar people; that ye should shew forth the praises of him who hath called you out of darkness into his marvellous light:

*Isaiah 46:10 - Declaring the end from the beginning, and from ancient times [the things] that are not [yet] done, saying, My counsel shall stand, and I will do all my pleasure:

*Revelation 4:11 - Thou art worthy, O Lord, to receive glory and honour and power: for thou hast created all things, and for thy pleasure they are and were created.

CHAPTER NINE
MANY PROMISES

According to one biblical source, there are over **7000** promises in the Bible. God has provided many prophetic promises to his people in order to meet every one of their needs. Of course this little book is only a small fraction of these promises that God has given to us. All the promises in **Christ** are yea and amen to the believer who would choose to believe what God says is true. This is one reason why we can cast all of our cares upon **him, because he cares for us**.

Blessings

*2 Corinthians 1:20 For all the promises of God in him are yea, and in him Amen, unto the glory of God by us.

---

*James 1:17 - Every good gift and every perfect gift is from above, and cometh down from the Father of lights, with whom is no variableness, neither shadow of turning.

---

*Luke 6:38 - Give, and it shall be given unto you; good measure, pressed down, and shaken together, and running over, shall men give into your bosom. For with the same measure that ye mete withal it shall be measured to you again.

---

*3 John 1:2 - Beloved, I wish above all things that thou mayest prosper and be in health, even as thy soul prospereth.

---

*Isaiah 41:10 - Fear thou not; for I [am] with thee: be not dismayed; for I [am] thy God: I will strengthen thee; yea, I will

help thee; yea, I will uphold thee with the right hand of my righteousness.

———————————————

*John 1:16 - And of his fulness have all we received, and grace for grace.

———————————————

*Philippians 2:13 - For it is God which worketh in you both to will and to do of [his] good pleasure.

———————————————

*2 Chronicles 27:6 - So Jotham became mighty, because he prepared his ways before the LORD his God.

———————————————

*Philippians 4:7 - And the peace of God, which passeth all understanding, shall keep your hearts and minds through Christ Jesus.

———————————————

*Philippians 1:6 - Being confident of this very thing, that he which hath begun a good work in you will perform [it] until the day of Jesus Christ:

———————————————

*2 Corinthians 9:8 And God [is] able to make all grace abound toward you; that ye, always having all sufficiency in all [things], may abound to every good work:

———————————————

*1 Corinthians 15:10 - But by the grace of God I am what I am: and his grace which [was bestowed] upon me was not in vain; but I laboured more abundantly than they all: yet not I, but the grace of God which was with me.

———————————————

*Matthew 24:13 - But he that shall endure unto the end, the same shall be saved.

———————————————

*Hebrews 10:36 - For ye have need of patience, that, after ye have done the will of God, ye might receive the promise.

Malachi 3:2 - But who may abide the day of his coming? and who shall stand when he appeareth? for he [is] like a refiner's fire, and like fullers' soap:

*Habakkuk 3:19 - The LORD God [is] my strength, and he will make my feet like hinds' [feet], and he will make me to walk upon mine high places.

*1 John 4:4 - Ye are of God, little children, and have overcome them: because greater is he that is in you, than he that is in the world.

*Ephesians 1:3 - Blessed [be] the God and Father of our Lord Jesus Christ, who hath blessed us with all spiritual blessings in heavenly [places] in Christ:

*Isaiah 1:19 - If ye be willing and obedient, ye shall eat the good of the land:

*Deuteronomy 28:1And it shall come to pass, if thou shalt hearken diligently unto the voice of the LORD thy God, to observe [and] to do all his commandments which I command thee this day, that the LORD thy God will set thee on high above all nations of the earth:

*Psalm 84:11 For the Lord God is a sun and shield: the Lord will give grace and glory: no good thing will he withhold from them that walk uprightly.

*James 1:18 - Of his own will begat he us with the word of truth, that we should be a kind of firstfruits of his creatures.

*2 Corinthians 10:4 - (For the weapons of our warfare [are] not carnal, but mighty through God to the pulling down of strong holds;)

---

*Zechariah 10:1 - Ask ye of the LORD rain in the time of the latter rain; [so] the LORD shall make bright clouds, and give them showers of rain, to every one grass in the field.

---

2 Thessalonians 1:7 And to you who are troubled rest with us, when the Lord Jesus shall be revealed from heaven with his mighty angels,8 In flaming fire taking vengeance on them that know not God, and that obey not the gospel of our Lord Jesus Christ:9 Who shall be punished with everlasting destruction from the presence of the Lord, and from the glory of his power;

Provision

*Deuteronomy 8:18 But thou shalt remember the Lord thy God: for it is he that giveth thee power to get wealth, that he may establish his covenant which he sware unto thy fathers, as it is this day.

---

*Proverbs 3:5 - Trust in the LORD with all thine heart; and lean not unto thine own understanding.

---

*Hebrews 13:5 - [Let your] conversation [be] without covetousness; [and be] content with such things as ye have: for he hath said, I will never leave thee, nor forsake thee.

---

*2 Peter 1:3 - According as his divine power hath given unto us all things that [pertain] unto life and godliness, through the knowledge of him that hath called us to glory and virtue:

---

*Philippians 1:6 - Being confident of this very thing, that he which hath begun a good work in you will perform [it] until the day of Jesus Christ:

---

*Matthew 11:28 - Come unto me, all [ye] that labour and are heavy laden, and I will give you rest.

---

*Philippians 2:12-13 - Wherefore, my beloved, as ye have always obeyed, not as in my presence only, but now much more in my absence, work out your own salvation with fear and trembling.

---

*2 Corinthians 5:21 - For he hath made him [to be] sin for us, who knew no sin; that we might be made the righteousness of God in him.

---

*Romans 3:23-26 - For all have sinned, and come short of the glory of God;

Overcomers In Christ

John 16:33 These things I have spoken unto you, that in me ye might have peace. In the world ye shall have tribulation: but be of good cheer; I have overcome the world.

Romans 12:21 Be not overcome of evil, but overcome evil with good.

---

2 Peter 2:20 For if after they have escaped the pollutions of the world through the knowledge of the Lord and Saviour Jesus Christ, they are again entangled therein, and overcome, the latter end is worse with them than the beginning.

1 John 5:3 For this is the love of God, that we keep his commandments: and his commandments are not grievous.4 For whatsoever is born of God overcometh the world: and this is the victory that overcometh the world, even our faith.5 Who is he that overcometh the world, but he that believeth that Jesus is the Son of God?

Revelation 2:7 He that hath an ear, let him hear what the Spirit saith unto the churches; To him that overcometh will I give to eat of the tree of life, which is in the midst of the paradise of God.

Revelation 2:11 He that hath an ear, let him hear what the Spirit saith unto the churches; He that overcometh shall not be hurt of the second death.

Revelation 2:17 He that hath an ear, let him hear what the Spirit saith unto the churches; To him that overcometh will I give to eat of the hidden manna, and will give him a white stone, and in the stone a new name written, which no man knoweth saving he that receiveth it.

Revelation 2:26 And he that overcometh, and keepeth my works unto the end, to him will I give power over the nations:

Revelation 3:5 He that overcometh, the same shall be clothed in white raiment; and I will not blot out his name out of the book of life, but I will confess his name before my Father, and before his angels.

Revelation 3:12 Him that overcometh will I make a pillar in the temple of my God, and he shall go no more out: and I will write upon him the name of my God, and the name of the city of my God, which is new Jerusalem, which cometh down out of heaven from my God: and I will write upon him my new name.

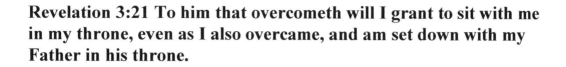

Revelation 3:21 To him that overcometh will I grant to sit with me in my throne, even as I also overcame, and am set down with my Father in his throne.

Revelation 11:7 And when they shall have finished their testimony, the beast that ascendeth out of the bottomless pit shall make war against them, and shall overcome them, and kill them.

Revelation 12:11 And they overcame him by the blood of the Lamb, and by the word of their testimony; and they loved not their lives unto the death.

Revelation 13:7 And it was given unto him to make war with the saints, and to overcome them: and power was given him over all kindreds, and tongues, and nations.

Revelation 17:14 These shall make war with the Lamb, and the Lamb shall overcome them: for he is Lord of lords, and King of kings: and they that are with him are called, and chosen, and faithful.

Revelation 21:7 He that overcometh shall inherit all things; and I will be his God, and he shall be my son.*Romans 12:21 Be not overcome of evil, but overcome evil with good.

*1 John 5:1-21 - Whosoever believeth that Jesus is the Christ is born of God: and every one that loveth him that begat loveth him also that is begotten of him.

*Matthew 7:21-23 - Not every one that saith unto me, Lord, Lord, shall enter into the kingdom of heaven; but he that doeth the will of my Father which is in heaven.

*1 John 5:3 - For this is the love of God, that we keep his commandments: and his commandments are not grievous.

*Hebrews 4:16 - Let us therefore come boldly unto the throne of grace, that we may obtain mercy, and find grace to help in time of need.

*John 12:31 - Now is the judgment of this world: now shall the prince of this world be cast out.

*Jeremiah 17:9 - The heart [is] deceitful above all [things], and desperately wicked: who can know it?

*Isaiah 55:7 - Let the wicked forsake his way, and the unrighteous man his thoughts: and let him return unto the LORD, and he will have mercy upon him; and to our God, for he will abundantly pardon.

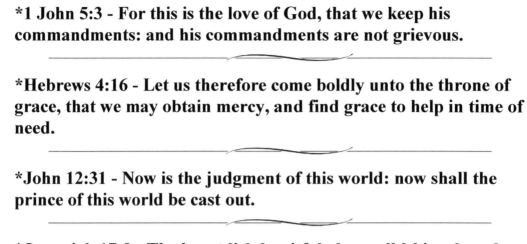

The Holiness of CHRIST

Mark 1:24 Saying, Let us alone; what have we to do with thee, thou Jesus of Nazareth? art thou come to destroy us? I know thee who thou art, the Holy One of God.

Romans 1:4 And declared to be the Son of God with power, according to the spirit of holiness, by the resurrection from the dead:

Acts 2:27 Because thou wilt not leave my soul in hell, neither wilt thou suffer thine Holy One to see corruption.

Acts 3:14 But ye denied the Holy One and the Just, and desired a murderer to be granted unto you;

Acts 13:35 Wherefore he saith also in another psalm, Thou shalt not suffer thine Holy One to see corruption.

1 John 2:20 But ye have an unction from the Holy One, and ye know all things.

Hebrews 9:14 How much more shall the blood of Christ, who through the eternal Spirit offered himself without spot to God, purge your conscience from dead works to serve the living God?

Exodus 15:11 Who is like unto thee, O Lord, among the gods? who is like thee, glorious in holiness, fearful in praises, doing wonders?

Psalm 47:8 God reigneth over the heathen: God sitteth upon the throne of his holiness.

Psalm 96:9 O worship the Lord in the beauty of holiness: fear before him, all the earth.

Isaiah 35:8 And an highway shall be there, and a way, and it shall be called The way of holiness; the unclean shall not pass over it; but it shall be for those: the wayfaring men, though fools, shall not err therein.

Romans 6:19 I speak after the manner of men because of the infirmity of your flesh: for as ye have yielded your members servants to uncleanness and to iniquity unto iniquity; even so now yield your members servants to righteousness unto holiness.

Romans 6:22 But now being made free from sin, and become servants to God, ye have your fruit unto holiness, and the end everlasting life.

2 Corinthians 7:1 Having therefore these promises, dearly beloved, let us cleanse ourselves from all filthiness of the flesh and spirit, perfecting holiness in the fear of God.

Ephesians 4:24 And that ye put on the new man, which after God is created in righteousness and true holiness.

1 Thessalonians 2:10 Ye are witnesses, and God also, how holily and justly and unblameably we behaved ourselves among you that believe:

1 Thessalonians 3:13 To the end he may stablish your hearts unblameable in holiness before God, even our Father, at the coming of our Lord Jesus Christ with all his saints.

1 Thessalonians 4:7 For God hath not called us unto uncleanness, but unto holiness.

Titus 2:3 The aged women likewise, that they be in behaviour as becometh holiness, not false accusers, not given to much wine, teachers of good things;

Hebrews 9:3 And after the second veil, the tabernacle which is called the Holiest of all;

Hebrews 9:8 The Holy Ghost this signifying, that the way into the holiest of all was not yet made manifest, while as the first tabernacle was yet standing:

Hebrews 10:19 Having therefore, brethren, boldness to enter into the holiest by the blood of Jesus,

Hebrews 12:10 For they verily for a few days chastened us after their own pleasure; but he for our profit, that we might be partakers of his holiness.

Hebrews 12:14 Follow peace with all men, and holiness, without which no man shall see the Lord:

The LAMB of GOD

John 1:29 The next day John seeth Jesus coming unto him, and saith, Behold the Lamb of God, which taketh away the sin of the world.

John 1:36 And looking upon Jesus as he walked, he saith, Behold the Lamb of God!

1 Peter 1:19 But with the precious blood of Christ, as of a lamb without blemish and without spot:20 Who verily was foreordained before the foundation of the world, but was manifest in these last times for you,

Revelation 5:6 And I beheld, and, lo, in the midst of the throne and of the four beasts, and in the midst of the elders, stood a Lamb as it had been slain, having seven horns and seven eyes, which are the seven Spirits of God sent forth into all the earth.

Revelation 7:10 And cried with a loud voice, saying, Salvation to our God which sitteth upon the throne, and unto the Lamb.

Revelation 7:17 For the Lamb which is in the midst of the throne shall feed them, and shall lead them unto living fountains of waters: and God shall wipe away all tears from their eyes.

Revelation 15:3 And they sing the song of Moses the servant of God, and the song of the Lamb, saying, Great and marvellous are thy works, Lord God Almighty; just and true are thy ways, thou King of saints.

Revelation 19:9 And he saith unto me, Write, Blessed are they which are called unto the marriage supper of the Lamb. And he saith unto me, These are the true sayings of God.

Revelation 21:22 And I saw no temple therein: for the Lord God Almighty and the Lamb are the temple of it.

Revelation 21:23 And the city had no need of the sun, neither of the moon, to shine in it: for the glory of God did lighten it, and the Lamb is the light thereof.

Revelation 22:1 And he shewed me a pure river of water of life, clear as crystal, proceeding out of the throne of God and of the Lamb.

Revelation 22:3 And there shall be no more curse: but the throne of God and of the Lamb shall be in it; and his servants shall serve him:

Isaiah 45:22 Look unto me, and be ye saved, all the ends of the earth: for I am God, and there is none else.

CHAPTER TEN
IMPORTANT SCRIPTURES

<u>*The Power of God's Word*</u>

Just this one particular subject alone could be never ending. There are many Scriptures dealing with the importance of the word. There are whole chapters that you and I could memorize and meditate upon, but that would be beyond the scope of this book. I will give to you what I would consider the most powerful Scriptures that are available dealing with God's word. Memorize these Scriptures and meditate upon them daily will surely bring an amazing change in your life in perspective.

*Hebrews 1:1 God, who at sundry times and in divers manners spake in time past unto the fathers by the prophets, 2 hath in these last days spoken unto us by his Son, whom he hath appointed heir of all things, by whom also he made the worlds; 3 who being the brightness of his glory, and the express image of his person, and upholding all things by the word of his power, when he had by himself purged our sins, sat down on the right hand of the Majesty on high; 4 Being made so much better than the angels, as he hath by inheritance obtained a more excellent name than they.5 For unto which of the angels said he at any time, Thou art my Son, this day have I begotten thee? And again, I will be to him a Father, and he shall be to me a Son?6 And again, when he bringeth in the firstbegotten into the world, he saith, And let all the angels of God worship him.7 And of the angels he saith, Who maketh his angels spirits, and his ministers a flame of fire.8 But unto the Son he saith, Thy throne, O God, is for ever and ever: a sceptre of righteousness is the sceptre of thy kingdom.9 Thou hast

loved righteousness, and hated iniquity; therefore God, even thy God, hath anointed thee with the oil of gladness above thy fellows.10 And, Thou, Lord, in the beginning hast laid the foundation of the earth; and the heavens are the works of thine hands:11 They shall perish; but thou remainest; and they all shall wax old as doth a garment;12 And as a vesture shalt thou fold them up, and they shall be changed: but thou art the same, and thy years shall not fail.13 But to which of the angels said he at any time, Sit on my right hand, until I make thine enemies thy footstool?14 Are they not all ministering spirits, sent forth to minister for them who shall be heirs of salvation?

*Hebrews 4:12 For the word of God is quick, and powerful, and sharper than any twoedged sword, piercing even to the dividing asunder of soul and spirit, and of the joints and marrow, and is a discerner of the thoughts and intents of the heart.

*Psalm 107:20 He sent his word, and healed them, and delivered them from their destructions.

*Luke 21:33 Heaven and earth shall pass away: but my words shall not pass away.

*Psalm 138:2 I will worship toward thy holy temple, and praise thy name for thy loving kindness and for thy truth: for thou hast magnified thy word above all thy name.

*Isaiah 55:11 so shall my word be that goeth forth out of my mouth: it shall not return unto me void, but it shall accomplish that which I please, and it shall prosper in the thing whereto I sent it.

*Isaiah 40:8 The grass withereth, the flower fadeth: but the word of our God shall stand for ever.

*1 Peter 1:25 But the word of the Lord endureth for ever.

*2 Timothy 3:16 All scripture [is] given by inspiration of God, and [is] profitable for doctrine, for reproof, for correction, for instruction in righteousness:

*Jeremiah 23:29 - [Is] not my word like as a fire? saith the LORD; and like a hammer [that] breaketh the rock in pieces?

*Psalms 119:105 Thy word [is] a lamp unto my feet, and a light unto my path.

*Ephesians 6:17 - And take the helmet of salvation, and the sword of the Spirit, which is the word of God:

*2 Corinthians 10:4 - (For the weapons of our warfare [are] not carnal, but mighty through God to the pulling down of strong holds;)

*Romans 10:17 - So then faith [cometh] by hearing, and hearing by the word of God.

*John 17:17 - Sanctify them through thy truth: thy word is truth.

*Matthew 4:4 - But he answered and said, It is written, Man shall not live by bread alone, but by every word that proceedeth out of the mouth of God.

*1 Peter 1:23 being born again, not of corruptible seed, but of incorruptible, by the word of God, which liveth and abideth for ever.

*1 Peter 2:2 as newborn babes, desire the sincere milk of the word, that ye may grow thereby:

Micah 7:18 Who is a God like unto thee, that pardoneth iniquity, and passeth by the transgression of the remnant of his heritage? he retaineth not his anger for ever, because he delighteth in mercy.

Luke 24:26 Ought not Christ to have suffered these things, and to enter into his glory?27 And beginning at Moses and all the prophets, he expounded unto them in all the scriptures the things concerning himself.

John 3:31 He that cometh from above is above all: he that is of the earth is earthly, and speaketh of the earth: he that cometh from heaven is above all.

John 8:23 And he said unto them, Ye are from beneath; I am from above: ye are of this world; I am not of this world.

Acts 3:15 And killed the Prince of life, whom God hath raised from the dead; whereof we are witnesses.

Acts 5:30 The God of our fathers raised up Jesus, whom ye slew and hanged on a tree.31 Him hath God exalted with his right hand to be a Prince and a Saviour, for to give repentance to Israel, and forgiveness of sins.32 And we are his witnesses of these things; and so is also the Holy Ghost, whom God hath given to them that obey him.

---

1 John 3:5 And ye know that he was manifested to take away our sins; and in him is no sin.

---

*Galatians 5:1 - Stand fast therefore in the liberty wherewith Christ hath made us free, and be not entangled again with the yoke of bondage.

Forgiveness

*Ephesians 4:32 - And be ye kind one to another, tenderhearted, forgiving one another, even as God for Christ's sake hath forgiven you.

*Mark 11:25 - And when ye stand praying, forgive, if ye have ought against any: that your Father also which is in heaven may forgive you your trespasses.

*1 John 1:9 - If we confess our sins, he is faithful and just to forgive us [our] sins, and to cleanse us from all unrighteousness.

*Matthew 6:14-15 - For if ye forgive men their trespasses, your heavenly Father will also forgive you:

*Matthew 7:21-23 - Not every one that saith unto me, Lord, Lord, shall enter into the kingdom of heaven; but he that doeth the will of my Father which is in heaven.

*2 Corinthians 7:1 - Having therefore these promises, dearly beloved, let us cleanse ourselves from all filthiness of the flesh and spirit, perfecting holiness in the fear of God.

Praise, Worship, Thanksgiving,

*Philippians 4:6 - Be careful for nothing; but in every thing by prayer and supplication with thanksgiving let your requests be made known unto God.

*Psalms 7:17 - I will praise the LORD according to his righteousness: and will sing praise to the name of the LORD most high.

*1 Thessalonians 5:18 - In every thing give thanks: for this is the will of God in Christ Jesus concerning you.

*Psalms 107:1 - O give thanks unto the LORD, for [he is] good: for his mercy [endureth] for ever.

*Ephesians 5:20 - Giving thanks always for all things unto God and the Father in the name of our Lord Jesus Christ;

*Psalms 50:14 - Offer unto God thanksgiving; and pay thy vows unto the most High:

*Psalms 100:1 Make a joyful noise unto the LORD, all ye lands.

*Hebrews 13:15 - By him therefore let us offer the sacrifice of praise to God continually, that is, the fruit of [our] lips giving thanks to his name.

*Luke 6:38 - Give, and it shall be given unto you; good measure, pressed down, and shaken together, and running over, shall men give into your bosom. For with the same measure that ye *Colossians 3:15 - And let the peace of God rule in your hearts, to the which also ye are called in one body; and be ye thankful.

*Habakkuk 3:17 - Although the fig tree shall not blossom, neither [shall] fruit [be] in the vines; the labour of the olive shall fail, and the fields shall yield no meat; the flock shall be cut off from the fold, and [there shall be] no herd in the stalls:

*Psalms 92:1[It is a] good [thing] to give thanks unto the LORD, and to sing praises unto thy name, O most High:

*1 Thessalonians 5:17 - Pray without ceasing.

*Psalms 95:6 - O come, let us worship and bow down: let us kneel before the LORD our maker.

*Matthew 18:20 - For where two or three are gathered together in my name, there am I in the midst of them.

*John 4:23 - But the hour cometh, and now is, when the true worshippers shall worship the Father in spirit and in truth: for the Father seeketh such to worship him.

*Psalms 29:2 - Give unto the LORD the glory due unto his name; worship the LORD in the beauty of holiness.

*1 Peter 2:5 - Ye also, as lively stones, are built up a spiritual house, an holy priesthood, to offer up spiritual sacrifices, acceptable to God by Jesus Christ.

*Psalms 96:9 - O worship the LORD in the beauty of holiness: fear before him, all the earth.

*Psalms 95:1-6 - O come, let us sing unto the LORD: let us make a joyful noise to the rock of our salvation.

*Psalms 96:8 - Give unto the LORD the glory [due unto] his name: bring an offering, and come into his courts.

*Acts 16:25 – And at midnight Paul and Silas prayed, and sang praises unto God: and the prisoners heard them.

The Fear of the Lord

*Philippians 2:12 Wherefore, my beloved, as ye have always obeyed, not as in my presence only, but now much more in my absence, work out your own salvation with fear and trembling.

*Proverbs 8:13 - The fear of the LORD [is] to hate evil: pride, and arrogancy, and the evil way, and the froward mouth, do I hate.

*Proverbs 1:7 - The fear of the LORD [is] the beginning of knowledge:

*Matthew 10:28 - And fear not them which kill the body, but are not able to kill the soul: but rather fear him which is able to destroy both soul and body in hell.

*Psalms 33:8 - Let all the earth fear the LORD: let all the inhabitants of the world stand in awe of him.

*Proverbs 14:27 - The fear of the LORD [is] a fountain of life, to depart from the snares of death.

*Psalms 25:14 - The secret of the LORD [is] with them that fear him; and he will shew them his covenant.

*Deuteronomy 10:12 - And now, Israel, what doth the LORD thy God require of thee, but to fear the LORD thy God, to walk in all his ways, and to love him, and to serve the LORD thy God with all thy heart and with all thy soul,

*Proverbs 16:6 - By mercy and truth iniquity is purged: and by the fear of the LORD [men] depart from evil.

---

*Psalms 19:9 - The fear of the LORD [is] clean, enduring for ever: the judgments of the LORD [are] true [and] righteous altogether.

---

*1 Peter 1:17 - And if ye call on the Father, who without respect of persons judgeth according to every man's work, pass the time of your sojourning [here] in fear:

---

*Ephesians 5:21 - Submitting yourselves one to another in the fear of God.

---

*Proverbs 14:16 - A wise [man] feareth, and departeth from evil: but the fool rageth, and is confident.

---

*2 Timothy 1:7 - For God hath not given us the spirit of fear; but of power, and of love, and of a sound mind.

Our Enemy the devil

*1 Peter 5:8 - Be sober, be vigilant; because your adversary the devil, as a roaring lion, walketh about, seeking whom he may devour:

---

*Hebrews 2:14 - Forasmuch then as the children are partakers of flesh and blood, he also himself likewise took part of the same; that through death he might destroy him that had the power of death, that is, the devil;

---

*2 Corinthians 11:14 - And no marvel; for Satan himself is transformed into an angel of light.

---

*2 Corinthians 10:3-5 - For though we walk in the flesh, we do not war after the flesh:

---

*Ephesians 6:12 For we wrestle not against flesh and blood, but against principalities, against powers, against the rulers of the darkness of this world, against spiritual wickedness in high places. 13 Wherefore take unto you the whole armour of God, that ye may be able to withstand in the evil day, and having done all, to stand.

---

*John 10:10 - The thief cometh not, but for to steal, and to kill, and to destroy: I am come that they might have life, and that they might have [it] more abundantly.

---

*John 8:44 - Ye are of [your] father the devil, and the lusts of your father ye will do. He was a murderer from the beginning, and abode not in the truth, because there is no truth in him. When he speaketh a lie, he speaketh of his own: for he is a liar, and the father of it.

Books Written by Doc Yeager:

"Living in the Realm of the Miraculous #1."
"I need God Cause I'm Stupid."
"The Miracles of Smith Wigglesworth"
"How Faith Comes 28 WAYS"
"Horrors of Hell, Splendors of Heaven"
"The Coming Great Awakening"
"Sinners in The Hands of an Angry GOD,"
"Brain Parasite Epidemic"
"My JOURNEY to HELL" - illustrated for teenagers
"Divine Revelation of Jesus Christ"
"My Daily Meditations"
"Holy Bible of JESUS CHRIST"
"War In The Heavenlies - (Chronicles of Micah)"
"Living in the Realm of the Miraculous #2."
"My Legal Rights to Witness"
"Why We (MUST) Gather! - 30 Biblical Reasons"
"My Incredible, Supernatural, Divine Experiences"
"Living in the Realm of the Miraculous #3."
"How GOD Leads & Guides! - 20 Ways"
"Weapons of Our Warfare"
"How You Can Be Healed"
"Hell Is For Real"
"Heaven Is For Real"
"God Still Heals"
"God Still Provides"
"God Still Protects"
"God Still Gives Dreams & Visions."
"God Still Does Miracles"
"God Still Gives Prophetic Words"
"God Still Confirms His Word With Power"
"Life Changing Quotes of Smith Wigglesworth"
"The Experts Handbook of Exorcism"

ABOUT THE AUTHOR

Dr. Michael and Kathleen Yeager have served as pastors/apostles, missionaries, evangelists, broadcasters, and authors for over four decades. They flow in the gifts of the Holy Spirit, teaching the Word of God with wonderful signs and miracles following in confirmation of God's Word. In 1983, they began Jesus is Lord Ministries International, Biglerville, PA 17307.

Websites Connected to Doc Yeager

www.docyeager.com

www.jilmi.org

www.wbntv.org

Made in the USA
Las Vegas, NV
02 December 2022

60940794R10085